Vol

MW01681458

CIVILIAN ORIENTATION MANUAL™

Recalibration in Civilian Systems

Applied Systems Transition℠ Framework

DR. PAUL ENCINIAS, EDD

Lightfoot Publishing LLC

Albuquerque, NM

Copyright © 2026 Paul Encinias
DR. PAUL ENCINIAS, EdD
CIVILIAN ORIENTATION MANUAL™
Recalibration in Civilian Systems™
All rights reserved.
Copyright registered with the U.S. Copyright Office

ISBN: 979-8-9966264-0-3 (print)
Library of Congress Control Number: 2026945942

No part of this publication may be reproduced, distributed, or transmitted in any form or by any means, including photocopying, recording, or other electronic or mechanical methods, without the prior written permission of the author, except in the case of brief quotations embodied in critical reviews and certain other non-commercial uses permitted by copyright law.

CIVILIAN ORIENTATION MANUAL™
Recalibration in Civilian Systems
Applied Systems Transition℠ Framework

DR. PAUL ENCINIAS, EdD
Lightfoot Publishing LLC

Printed Worldwide
First Printing 2026
First Edition 2026

10 9 8 7 6 5 4 3 2 1

Interior Book Design by Walt's Book Design
www.waltsbookdesign.com

CIVILIAN ORIENTATION MANUAL

This book is dedicated to every veteran who has navigated this transition—and to the ones who did not make it through. To those who paid the ultimate price in service, and to those who were lost in the years after, when the mission was over but the weight of it was not. You are not forgotten.

To the families who stood beside them through the deployments, the moves, the uncertainty, and the long work of coming home. And to the families who carry that loss forward every day. This book is for you too.

If this work reaches one veteran at the right moment—if it pulls one person back from the edge or gives one family a language for what they are living through—then it has done what it was built to do. I have spent over a decade making sacrifices to build this. If it saves one life, every one of those sacrifices was worth it.

Notices and Limitations

This manual provides general information, frameworks, and practical guidance only. It does not constitute legal, financial, medical, or professional advice and does not replace individualized counseling or official determinations made by government agencies or employers. Benefits programs, laws, policies, and organizational practices may change over time, vary by location, or depend on individual circumstances. Readers are responsible for verifying current requirements and making decisions appropriate to their own situation.

Non-Endorsement

This publication is not affiliated with, endorsed by, or sponsored by the US Department of Defense, the Department of Veterans Affairs, or any other government agency. References to military practices, government programs, standards, or organizations are provided for informational and educational purposes only. The views expressed are those of the author and do not represent official policy or positions of any government entity. Distribution does not imply endorsement by any government agency.

Updates and Revisions

Information affecting veterans, including benefits, employment programs, and economic conditions, evolves over time. This manual may be updated to reflect changes, improve clarity, or incorporate better explanations as new information becomes available. Readers are encouraged to consult the most current edition when making important decisions.

Use and handling

Distribution of this publication is permitted only by organizations granted written authorization by Lightfoot Publishing LLC. Authorized distribution is limited to non-commercial educational use. Alteration, adaptation, or creation of derivative works requires prior written permission from the publisher. This publication contains original intellectual property authored by Dr. Paul Encinias, EdD. All framework methodology and content remain the exclusive property of the author and publisher.

Pronoun Usage

For readability, this publication may use the terms "he," "him," "his," or "her" when referring to individuals. These terms are intended to be inclusive of all persons and do not denote gender preference or exclusion.

*"Most people do not fail because they lack effort.
They fail because they misunderstood the system they are operating in."*

— Dr. Paul Encinias

TABLE OF CONTENTS

NOTE FROM THE AUTHOR

This manual was not written from the outside.

I served four years on active duty in the United States Navy, deploying in support of Operation Enduring Freedom. When I separated, my transition went wrong. Not gradually but quickly, and in ways that the standard explanations did not account for. The resources available at the time told me what to do. None of them explained what I was actually dealing with.

I entered entrepreneurship because it was the only viable path available after being let go from a civilian position. The business grew. I expanded across multiple states. And then it failed. What followed was the hardest period of my life: a bankruptcy and a collapse that took everything I had built. I was homeless at one point. The explanations I had been given for why the transition from the military to civilian life was hard did not come close to accounting for what had actually happened to me.

Rather than accept those explanations, I went back to find different ones.

That search became a decade of formal research. I earned a Doctor of Education in Organizational Leadership from the University of Massachusetts Global and an MBA with a concentration in international business. I also completed advanced graduate studies in executive and nonprofit leadership. I am currently attending Law School, pursuing a Master of Legal Studies in Litigation. My doctoral dissertation examined how post-9/11 veterans navigate civilian employment and is among the first formal research studies to document the structural gap between military and civilian systems.

That sequence matters. The framework in this manual was not built in a library. It was built by someone who fell through every layer of the transition problem, documented what he found, and then spent years developing a structured system to make sure the next veteran has something he never did: a way to read the environment before walking into it.

Currently, I am working as a quality management systems architect, designing structured systems that connect organizational processes, decision-making, and performance outcomes. I have extensive experience in government procurement.

My work has been recognized by the Department of the Navy, the United States Senate, the California State Legislature, the University of California Merced, the SBDC Regional Network, flag admirals, commanding officers, and other institutional leaders. I also hold a Certificate of Special Congressional Recognition.

A central purpose of my work is to use my education and personal experience to develop programs that support veterans during their transition to civilian life and help reduce the conditions that can lead to crises and, in the worst-case scenario, suicide. I have seen where the gap leads when it goes unaddressed. That is why this manual exists.

This manual was written from the position of a free agent: no government affiliation. No institutional contract. No obligation to any program, agency, or employer. That independence is not incidental. It is what makes an honest account of these systems possible.

Dr. Paul Encinias, EdD

US Navy Veteran

INTRODUCTION

The military trained you to operate inside one of the rarest institutional structures on earth. When you separated, you did not step into a civilian version of that system. You stepped into hundreds of systems: each one partial, each one inconsistent, each one operating under rules that were never made explicit. This book gives you the framework to read those systems before you make decisions inside them.

The military made you exceptionally good at operating inside a system. It just never told you that is what it was doing.

It also never told you something more important: The system you were trained in is one of the rarest institutional structures on earth. Fully unified authority. Predefined roles at every level. Evaluation criteria that exist before the mission starts. Risk absorbed by the institution, not the individual. A handful of militaries operate this way. A handful of the largest organizations in the world come close. That is the full list.

When you separated, you did not step into a civilian version of that system. You stepped into something no one prepared you for. Not a single system operating under different rules but hundreds of systems, each one partial, each one inconsistent, each one trying in its own way to achieve the kind of coherence you already lived inside for years. Some come close. Most do not.

Some of them connect through contracts, partnerships, and supply chains. A prime contractor and its subcontractor can look unified from the outside: coordinated, structured, pointed in the same direction. But coordination is different from unity. A prime and its subs are not operating inside the same system. They are operating inside adjacent systems, each with its own authority structure, its own risk distribution, its own rules, temporarily aligned by a contract that has an end date. When that contract ends, the alignment ends with it.

The organizations you have been walking into since you separated are not a looser version of what you left. They are fragments. And you have been applying the skills of someone trained in a complete, unified system to environments that were never built to receive them.

That is why the effort stopped converting. That is why the leadership that worked in uniform started generating friction. That is why the process discipline that made you effective started being called inflexible. It was not you. It was a collision between what you were built for and what actually exists out there.

Nobody told you that on your way out. Nobody in any transition program said, "The world you are entering does not have one system; it has hundreds, and most of them are incomplete." Nobody handed you a way to read those systems before you walked into them and started making decisions.

That is what this book does.

The explanation most veterans receive (from well-meaning people on all sides) is a behavioral one. You need to translate your experience better. You need to communicate differently. You need to be more flexible, more patient, more civilian. The problem, in this explanation, lies with you.

That explanation is incomplete. And in many cases, it is wrong.

Research into how post-9/11 veterans navigate civilian employment reveals something that behavioral explanations consistently miss. Veterans leaving military service are not simply moving from one job to another. They are exiting one of the most highly bounded institutional systems in modern society and entering a fragmented civilian environment that operates under fundamentally different structural rules: rules that are rarely made explicit, rarely consistent, and rarely designed with any awareness of what veterans were trained to expect.

The friction is not personal. It is structural.

That distinction matters more than it might appear to at first. If the problem is behavioral, the solution is behavioral. Change how you present yourself, communicate, and adapt. If the problem is structural, the solution is structural. Learn to read the environment you are actually in before you decide how to operate within it.

Most of the resources available to veterans address the first problem.

This book addresses the second.

◆ ◆ ◆

Here Is What This Book Is

It is a diagnostic tool. Not a motivational resource. Not a career guide. Not a collection of success stories from veterans who figured it out. Those books exist. This is not one of them.

What you will find here is a framework for reading civilian environments before you make decisions inside them. The framework is called the Applied Systems Transition Framework (AST), and it rests on a single organizing principle: The structural conditions of the environment you are in determine the outcomes you can expect from it, independent of your capability, your effort, or your motivation.

In plain terms, the same veteran doing the same work with the same level of effort will produce different outcomes in different structural environments. Not because they changed. Because the system changed.

Once you can classify the environment before you invest in it, you stop misreading system-produced outcomes as personal failures. You start making decisions based on what is actually true about the environment in front of you.

That applies whether you are about to take your first civilian job, whether you have been out for years and are still trying to find solid ground, or whether you are sitting in a job right now wondering why your performance is not translating into what it should. It applies whether you just got out last month or separated a decade ago, and the friction never fully went away. It applies if you are thinking about starting your own business—drawn to the ownership, the autonomy, the idea of building something on your own terms, but something is telling you to understand the landscape before you step into it.

The structural problem does not care how long you have been out. It is present in every civilian environment you will ever enter. What changes is your ability to see it.

◆ ◆ ◆

Taylor

Throughout this book, you will follow Taylor.

Taylor is not a real person. Taylor has no branch, no MOS, no rate, no AFSC. Taylor has no rank, no years of service, and no specific deployment history. Taylor's competence and effort never change across any of the examples in this book.

What changes is the system Taylor is operating in.

That is the point. Taylor exists to make structural effects visible in a way that individual stories cannot. When you read about Taylor getting passed over for a promotion despite clear performance, the story is not about Taylor's shortcomings. It is about what kind of system Taylor was in and whether that system had the architecture to recognize and reward what Taylor was doing.

You will recognize situations Taylor encounters. Some of them will be uncomfortably familiar. That is intentional.

◆ ◆ ◆

What This Book Delivers

It does not tell you what decision to make. It does not recommend specific employers, specific career paths, or specific transition timelines. It does not make promises about outcomes.

What it does is give you the ability to look at any civilian environment: a job posting, a company, a small business, a federal agency, a startup, a role you are already sitting in. It gives you the ability to identify its structural conditions accurately. That is a capability most veterans never develop because no one ever explained that it was necessary.

Most veterans have access to the resources necessary for important tasks. Resume writing, interview technique, benefits navigation—those things matter, and they help. But they address the surface of the transition problem, not the root of it.

The root of it is that veterans are trained to operate inside a system that civilian environments do not replicate. When that system disappears, the skills remain. But the environment that made those skills legible is gone. What veterans need is not more behavioral coaching. What they need is the ability to read whatever environment has replaced the one they left.

That ability does not expire. It is just as useful five years out as it is five days out. It is just as useful when you are evaluating a new job offer as it is when you are trying to understand why the job you are already in feels wrong.

◆ ◆ ◆

The One Idea This Book Delivers

By the time you finish this book, you will be able to do one thing you could not do before you started.

You will be able to look at any civilian environment and classify it accurately: where authority actually lives, how roles are actually defined, how risk is actually distributed, and what that means for what you can expect from operating inside it.

That is not everything. It is not meant to be.

◆ ◆ ◆

Three Volumes

This is Volume I of a three-part system. Each volume builds on the one before it, but each one also stands on its own.

Volume I (what you are holding) gives you the diagnostic foundation. By the end of it, you will be able to classify any civilian environment accurately. That is the only goal of this book. Volume II takes that foundation and applies it to the specific decisions most veterans face: resumes, job postings, interviews, income translation, and career placement. Once you can read an environment, Volume II gives you the tools to move through it.

Volume III is the complete manual. Not a longer book but a different category of document entirely. It is a structured reference system built the way high-functioning organizations build their own internal doctrine: cross-referenced, indexed, and designed to be consulted under real conditions rather than read once and set aside. Every domain a veteran encounters across a full transition and beyond is covered: benefits, family systems, entrepreneurship, federal contracting, income, purpose, debt, retirement. Each one is analyzed through the same diagnostic framework; each one is connected to the others. It contains scoring instruments, decision frameworks, and diagnostic tools designed to be referenced at the moment of decision, not studied in advance. Veterans from the most structured military environments will recognize the architecture immediately. It was built to match the standard they were trained to expect.

You do not need Volume II or Volume III to get value from this book. This is where the system starts. If what you read here changes how you see the civilian world—and it will—you will know where to go next.

Let us start.

The research underlying the Applied Systems Transition framework draws on a phenomenological study of post-9/11 US military veterans navigating civilian employment, as well as the organizational quality management literature tracing the structural lineage between military institutional systems and civilian organizational frameworks. Where research findings are referenced throughout this book, they reflect documented patterns across veteran populations, not individual anecdotes dressed up as data.

PART ONE

The System You Came From

CHAPTER 1

THE SYSTEM YOU CAME FROM

The military is a structural environment: one built around explicit authority, predefined roles, institutional risk absorption, and evaluation criteria that exist before the work begins. You were trained inside that system for years. What it gave you, it gave you without explanation. This chapter describes that system plainly so that what comes next has a foundation to stand on.

Nobody told you what kind of system you were in.

That is not a criticism. It is simply true. The military does not describe itself in structural terms; it does not hand you a briefing on its own architecture when you arrive. You learn it by operating inside it. You learn where decisions live by watching what happens when one needs to be made. You learn what your role is by doing it, and doing it again, until the boundaries are clear, not because someone explained them but because the work made them visible. You learn what happens when something goes wrong by watching the institution respond: absorbing, correcting, continuing.

You were trained inside one of the most structurally defined systems that exists anywhere. You just never had occasion to call it that.

This chapter gives it a name.

What the Military Actually Built

The military was built to function under conditions that would break most organizations. Incomplete information. Extreme time pressure. Consequences that are not abstract. That design requirement (operate effectively even when the situation is unclear, even when people change, even when everything goes wrong at once) shaped every structural feature of the institution.

Start with authority. In the military, authority is explicit. You know who owns a decision. You know who can override it. You know what happens when the person at the top of a decision chain is unavailable because the system has already accounted for that. The chain does not depend on any particular person being present. It depends on the chain itself existing, being documented, and being understood by everyone operating inside it. Authority is not a product of personality or relationships or whoever happens to be in the room. It is an architectural feature of the organization.

Roles work the same way. Before you arrived at any assignment, the position existed. It had documented responsibilities. It connected to other positions through established relationships that did not require you to build them from scratch. You did not have to figure out what you were supposed to be doing; the role told you, and the institution reinforced it. The boundaries of your job were not something you negotiated. They were established before you walked in.

Risk operated at the institutional level. When something went wrong—and things went wrong, as they go wrong everywhere—the organization had mechanisms to absorb it. Corrective action processes. Oversight structures. Formal review cycles. Not because the institution was trying to protect individuals from accountability, but because diffusing risk across the system rather than concentrating it on individuals is how you keep an organization functional under pressure. The institution was designed to catch errors before they became catastrophes. That design was deliberate.

Evaluation criteria existed before the work began. You knew what superior performance looked like before the mission started, not because someone told you once and expected you to remember but because the standards were documented, referenced, and applied consistently across every cycle. The performance review was not a surprise. The criteria were not invented after the fact. The system told you in advance what it was measuring, and then it measured it.

None of this happened because of any individual commander or any particular unit. It happened because the institution was designed to produce those conditions regardless of who was inside it. The authority structure, the role definitions, the risk absorption, the evaluation framework—those were features of the system itself, not of the people running it.

What That Structure Did for You—Without Telling You

When you are inside a system, you do not experience it as a system. You experience it as the way things work.

You experienced clear authority not as a structural feature but as a daily operational reality: Someone owns this decision, here is who it is, here is how to reach them. You experienced predefined roles not as an architectural choice but as the simple fact of knowing what your job was before you showed up to do it. You experienced institutional risk absorption not as a policy but as the knowledge that when something went wrong, there was a process for addressing it that did not begin and end with you personally.

You experienced evaluation not as a performance management system but as the steady presence of standards: criteria that existed before the work started, that applied to everyone operating at your level, that connected what you did to what the institution valued in a way that was traceable and consistent.

That structure was doing something for you. It was converting your effort into outcomes in a way that was legible to you, to the people evaluating you, to the organization as a whole. When you worked hard and performed well, the system had mechanisms to recognize and reward that. When you led people effectively, the organization had a way to see it. When you built something—a process, a capability, a team that functioned—the institution had the structural continuity to preserve it after you moved on.

You did not have to build any of that infrastructure. It was already there.

This is not a small thing. Most of the people and organizations in the world do not operate inside a structure that provides those conditions. The clarity of authority, the definition of roles, the institutional absorption of risk, the existence of evaluation criteria in advance—in most civilian environments, those things range from partially present to entirely absent. The military's version of them is not the norm. It is the exception.

You were trained inside the exception. And no one told you that it was exceptional.

◆ ◆ ◆

Taylor in Uniform

Here, Taylor is a logistics and operations specialist working in uniform. The branch does not matter. The years of service do not matter. What matters is this: Taylor is good at the work, and inside the system Taylor was trained in, that goodness is visible.

Taylor operates inside a structure where the mission is clear before it begins. The role is defined: not loosely, not aspirationally, but specifically, with documented responsibilities that existed before Taylor arrived. Authority is traceable at every level of the organization. When a decision needs to be made, Taylor knows who owns it. When Taylor owns a decision, the scope of that ownership is understood by everyone involved.

When something goes wrong (a supply chain disruption, an equipment failure, a coordination gap between units), there is a process for addressing it. Taylor does not absorb that failure alone. The institution has mechanisms. Corrective action. Review cycles. Oversight structures that exist specifically to catch problems before they compound. Taylor is accountable for the work. The institution carries a share of the risk.

When Taylor performs well, the system can see it. Standards were defined before the evaluation cycle began. Taylor knows what the criteria are. The people evaluating Taylor know what the criteria are. The connection between performance and outcome—recognition, advancement, continued responsibility—is not invisible or arbitrary. It runs through a documented process that applies consistently across everyone at Taylor's level.

Taylor works hard, performs well, and the effort converts. Not perfectly. No system is perfect. But consistently, in a way that is traceable from input to output.

Taylor does not think of any of this as unusual. It is simply how things work.

Rarer Than You Realize

When you separated, you carried everything the system gave you: the competence, the discipline, the ability to operate under pressure, the habits of mind that years of structured service build. Those things are real, and they are yours.

What you may not have carried with you, because no one said it plainly, is an understanding of the environment those capabilities were built inside.

The authority structure you operated within—explicit, traceable, functioning—is not how most organizations are built. The role definition you took for granted—predefined, documented, connected to the work—is not something most civilian employees encounter when they start a new job. The institutional risk absorption that kept individual exposure bounded—the processes, the oversight, the corrective mechanisms—is not a feature of most civilian workplaces. The evaluation criteria that existed before your performance was assessed—the standards you knew in advance, applied consistently, and connected to documented outcomes—are not the norm outside the military context.

These are not minor differences. They are fundamental ones. They are the difference between an organization built to function regardless of who is inside it and organizations built for entirely different purposes under entirely different constraints.

A handful of militaries on Earth operate the way the military operates. A handful of the largest, most regulated civilian organizations have developed structural features that approach it in some domains. That is the full list.

Every other organization you will ever enter was built differently.

Not worse. Not broken. Differently. For different purposes, under different pressures, toward different ends. Understanding that difference is what the rest of this book is about. But the first step is understanding what you actually came from.

You came from one of the most structurally defined environments on earth. Most veterans leave without being told that. Now you have been.

◆ ◆ ◆

What Comes Next

Knowing what the military is, structurally, is the starting point. The next step is understanding what changes when you leave it. Not the culture, not the mission, not the people. The infrastructure. The way authority works, how coordination moves, how continuity is maintained, and how evaluation operates in environments that were built under completely different constraints than the one you came from.

That is what the next chapter covers.

CHAPTER 2

INFRASTRUCTURE DIVERGENCE: WHY CIVILIAN SYSTEMS FEEL DIFFERENT

Military and civilian systems were built for fundamentally different purposes under fundamentally different constraints. The divergence between veterans' experiences is structural, not cultural. It shows up predictably in how authority is located, how coordination moves, how continuity is maintained, and how feedback operates. Neither system is wrong. Understanding the structural difference is not about judging civilian organizations. It is about reading them accurately before making decisions inside them.

There is a moment most veterans recognize.

It happens somewhere in the first civilian job, or the second, or the third. You are in a meeting, or waiting on a decision, or watching a process unfold in a way that would have looked completely different where you came from. And you have the same thought every time: This should not be this hard.

Not because the work is difficult. You have done challenging work. Not because the people are incompetent. Some of them are exceptional. But something underneath the organization—something in the structure itself—is operating differently from what you were trained in. Decisions move on a different timeline. Authority works through different channels. The process that exists on paper connects to the actual work in ways that are not always visible from the outside.

You adjust. You compensate. You try to apply what worked before because that is what capable people do when they encounter unfamiliar conditions.

And sometimes it works. And sometimes you get told you are making things more complicated than they need to be.

This chapter explains what is actually happening in that moment. Not the cultural explanation. Not the personality explanation. The structural one.

◆ ◆ ◆

Two Systems Built for Completely Different Purposes

The military was not designed to generate profit, attract customers, or compete in a market. It was designed to absorb uncertainty at an institutional level to function under conditions of incomplete information, extreme pressure, and potentially catastrophic consequences. Every structural feature of military organization traces back to that design requirement.

Explicit authority chains exist because, in conditions of uncertainty, someone has to be able to decide without convening a committee. Predefined roles exist because when the situation changes faster than communication allows, everyone needs to know their job without being told. Documented processes exist because institutional knowledge cannot live only in the heads of the people currently holding the positions. Risk absorption exists at the institutional level because individual exposure in high-stakes environments produces paralysis, not performance.

The military was built the way it was built because the consequences of structural failure are catastrophic. That is not a value judgment. It is an engineering decision.

Civilian organizations were built under completely different constraints. Most of them were built to generate value (profit, services, outcomes) in a competitive environment where the primary pressure is economic, not operational. Their structural features trace back to that design requirement.

Authority in civilian organizations is often distributed and relational because that model routes decisions efficiently through the people with the most relevant knowledge, regardless of title. Roles are often defined broadly because flexibility is a competitive advantage when market conditions shift. Processes are often carried in institutional knowledge rather than documentation because lean operations move faster. Risk is distributed across individuals and teams in ways that align personal accountability with organizational outcomes.

Civilian organizations were built the way they were built because the structural model that serves an economic environment is fundamentally different from the one that serves an operational one. That is also not a value judgment. It is also an engineering decision.

Neither system is wrong. They were built for different purposes under different pressures. The friction veterans experience is not evidence that one system is better than the other. It is evidence that two systems built under completely distinctive design requirements produce different structural behaviors and that moving between them without a way to read those differences creates confusion.

Where the Divergence Becomes Visible

The gap between military and civilian infrastructure does not announce itself. It shows up in specific, predictable places—the same places, in organization after organization, across industries, across roles, across every tier of the civilian economy. Once you know where to look, you will recognize it consistently.

Authority

In the military, authority is explicit and traceable. You know who owns a decision. You know who can override it. You know what happens when the chain is broken. That clarity is a functional requirement for an organization operating under time pressure with high-stakes outcomes.

In civilian organizations, authority operates differently. It is often distributed across roles, relationships, and levels of the organization in ways that reflect the actual flow of knowledge and decision-making rather than a fixed hierarchy. The person with the title does not always own the decision. The person without the title sometimes does. Authority moves based on context, expertise, relationships, and organizational dynamics that are understood by the people inside the system, even when they are not written down.

For veterans trained to locate authority precisely and act within it clearly, entering an environment where authority operates through different channels produces a specific kind of friction, not because the civilian system is broken but because the signals that communicate authority look completely different than the ones you were trained to read.

Coordination

In the military, coordination is structured through specific mechanisms—briefings, orders, after-action reviews, communication protocols—that exist to align action across people and units operating under time pressure. Those mechanisms were designed because the consequences of misalignment can be severe.

In civilian organizations, coordination operates differently. It moves through relationships, conversations, email chains, and meetings that often serve as much as alignment tools as they do decision-making forums. There is no equivalent of a five-paragraph order. Not because civilian organizations do not coordinate, but because the speed, flexibility, and relational nature of civilian coordination serve economic environments in ways that formal mechanisms would slow down.

For veterans trained to coordinate through structured processes, entering an environment where coordination is relational and informal means learning to read a separate set of signals: not a lesser set, just a different one.

Continuity

In the military, institutional continuity is a design requirement. Turnover is built into the system. When a commanding officer rotates out, the unit continues to function because processes, documentation, and institutional knowledge are embedded in the organization, not in the individual. The system was designed to outlast any single person inside it.

In civilian organizations, continuity is maintained differently. Institutional knowledge often lives in the people who hold it: in the relationships they have built, the processes they have developed, and the organizational history they carry. This is not a design flaw. In many environments, it is an efficient model that concentrates expertise where it is most useful and keeps organizations lean. But it means that continuity depends on people in ways that military systems were specifically designed to avoid.

For veterans trained to expect institutional continuity that is independent of individuals, entering an environment where continuity is person-carried means operating with a separate set of assumptions about how knowledge and process are preserved and what happens when key people move.

Feedback

In the military, feedback is structured, regular, and tied directly to performance standards defined in advance. You know what good looks like before the mission starts. After-action reviews happen whether things went well or not. Feedback is a functional requirement for an organization that needs to improve continuously under high-stakes conditions.

In civilian organizations, feedback operates on a different rhythm and through different mechanisms. Formal reviews may happen annually. Real-time feedback often moves through informal channels—a conversation, a reaction, a pattern of decisions made around you rather than with you. Standards are often defined through outcomes rather than in advance. This model gives civilian organizations flexibility to evaluate performance in context rather than against a fixed rubric, which serves dynamic environments well.

For veterans trained to receive structured, standards-based feedback on a regular cycle, entering an environment where feedback is contextual and informal means learning to read a different kind of signal and understanding that the absence of formal feedback is different from the absence of evaluation.

◆ ◆ ◆

This Is Not About Culture

The explanation most veterans receive for this friction is a cultural one. Military culture is different from civilian culture. You need to adapt. You need to learn to operate in a less structured environment. You need to be more flexible.

That explanation points at something real. But it often misidentifies the source.

Culture is the surface. Infrastructure is underneath it. When a civilian organization feels different from what you trained inside, that feeling is not primarily a cultural signal; it is a structural one. The organization operates differently because its authority is distributed differently, its coordination moves through different channels, its continuity is maintained differently, and its feedback operates on a different rhythm. Those are infrastructure conditions. They reflect deliberate design choices made for legitimate reasons—not deficiencies, not failures, not evidence that the organization is poorly run.

Understanding the difference between a cultural explanation and a structural one matters because the responses are different. If the problem is cultural, the response is adaptation: Change how you present yourself and how you communicate. If the difference is structural, the response is classification: Identify what kind of infrastructure you are actually operating inside so you can engage with it accurately rather than through the lens of a system it was never designed to be.

A veteran who reads structural differences as cultural failures may spend years trying to change their behavior in response to conditions that their behavior was never the cause of. A veteran who reads structural conditions accurately can engage with any environment on its own terms and make informed decisions about where to invest effort and where not to.

◆ ◆ ◆

Taylor in Two Environments

Taylor is a logistics coordinator. The branch does not matter. The years of service do not matter. What matters is this: By every structural measure the military provided, Taylor performed exceptionally. Authority was clear. Roles were defined. Performance standards existed before the mission started. Taylor operated inside that system and delivered results consistently.

Taylor separates and takes a logistics role at a mid-sized distribution company. The title is similar. The work is similar. The competence Taylor brings is identical to what produced exceptional performance in uniform.

Six months in, the results do not match the effort.

Decisions that Taylor expected to move in a day move in two weeks because authority over those decisions is distributed across three people whose roles overlap in ways that were never formally defined. Processes that Taylor was told exist turn out to be carried primarily by one person who has been with the company for fifteen years and coordinates largely through relationships built over that time. Coordination between departments happens through channels that Taylor has not yet been brought into. Feedback comes once at a ninety-day check-in that covered the basics but did not connect Taylor's specific performance to any defined standard.

Taylor adjusts. Works harder. Tries to build clearer processes. Documents workflows. Creates structure where the structure is not yet visible.

And gets told by a manager, "You are making things more complicated than they need to be."

Nothing about Taylor changed between the uniform and this job. Taylor's competence, effort, and judgment are identical. What changed is the structural environment Taylor is now operating inside. Authority is distributed differently. Coordination moves through different channels. Continuity is carried by people rather than embedded in systems. Feedback operates on a different rhythm.

Taylor is not failing. Taylor is operating inside a system that works differently from the one Taylor was trained in and trying to apply the logic of one system to the conditions of another.

That is what this chapter is about. Not how to judge either system. Not how to change either system. How to see the difference—clearly, accurately—so that the next environment you enter gets read on its own terms before effort goes into it.

◆ ◆ ◆

What Comes Next

Knowing that military and civilian infrastructure diverge is the first step. The second step is understanding that civilian infrastructure is not uniform. It varies significantly from one organization to the next. Some civilian environments are built with high structural coherence. Some operate with a moderate amount of structure that is applied unevenly. Some have almost no stable structure at all.

That variation is not random. It follows observable patterns. It is classifiable. And the next chapter introduces the framework that makes that classification possible so that any environment, in any industry, at any stage of your transition, can be read accurately before you decide how to engage with it.

PART TWO

The Tier Framework

CHAPTER 3

THE BIG PICTURE: CIVILIAN ORGANIZATIONS AS SYSTEMS

◆ ◆ ◆

Civilian organizations vary significantly in their degree of structural containment—how explicitly authority is defined, how clearly roles are established, how risk is distributed, and how evaluation criteria are set. That variation follows observable patterns organized into three tiers: Tier 1 environments are bounded and structurally coherent; Tier 2 environments have partial and uneven structure; Tier 3 environments—The Nothing—have no stable organizational structure at all. The tier framework is a classification tool, not a judgment system. Its purpose is to give veterans an accurate reading of any environment before making decisions inside it.

◆ ◆ ◆

Key Terms

Structural containment: The degree to which an organization provides predefined roles, codified authority, consistent evaluation criteria, and institutional risk absorption.

Tier 1 (Bounded): A civilian environment with explicit authority, predefined roles, advanced evaluation criteria, and significant institutional risk absorption. The most structurally coherent civilian tier.

Tier 2 (Unbounded): A civilian environment with partial or unevenly applied structure. Authority, roles, and evaluation exist but operate inconsistently.

Tier 3 (The Nothing): The absence of organizational structure. No stable authority, predefined roles, advanced evaluation, or institutional risk absorption. Early-stage entrepreneurship is the clearest example.

◆ ◆ ◆

Not every civilian environment feels the same. You may know this. Or you may one day.

You may have felt it in the difference between a federal agency and a startup. Between a large corporation and a three-person consulting firm. Between a job where everything had a process and a job where nothing did. Between an environment where your first week included structured onboarding and a clear role, and one where you showed up on Monday and spent the first month figuring out what you were actually supposed to be doing.

Most people attribute that difference to industry. Or company culture. Or management style. Or luck.

Those things matter. But they are not the primary driver of what you were actually feeling.

What you were feeling was structural containment—the degree to which an organization provides predefined roles, codified authority, consistent evaluation, and institutional risk absorption. Some environments have it in abundance. Some have it partially and unevenly. Some have almost none of it at all.

That variation is not random. It is not industry-specific. It is not a function of how good the leadership is or how long the company has been around. It follows observable structural patterns that show up consistently across every sector, every size, and every type of civilian organization.

This chapter gives you the framework to see those patterns—and name them—before you walk into any environment and start making decisions inside it.

◆ ◆ ◆

What Structural Containment Actually Means

Before the framework can be useful, the concept underneath it needs to be clear.

Structural containment is not about whether an organization is well-run. It is not about whether the people are competent, whether the culture is positive, or whether the work is meaningful. An organization can be excellently managed and have low structural containment. An organization can be poorly managed and have high structural containment. The two are related, but they are not the same thing.

Structural containment is specifically about four observable conditions.

Where authority lives

In a highly contained environment, authority is explicit. You can trace who owns a decision, who can override it, and what happens when the chain breaks. In a less contained environment, authority is distributed, informal, and contextual. It moves based on relationships, expertise, and organizational dynamics that are understood internally but rarely documented.

How roles are defined

In a highly contained environment, roles are predefined. Before you start the job, the job exists—with documented responsibilities, clear boundaries, and established expectations. In a less contained environment, roles are defined through the work itself. They emerge over time, shift based on organizational need, and often depend heavily on the person occupying them.

How risk is distributed

In a highly contained environment, the institution absorbs a significant portion of risk. If something goes wrong, the organization has mechanisms (processes, oversight, corrective action) that exist to catch and correct it before it becomes catastrophic. In a less contained environment, risk sits closer to the individual. When something goes wrong, the exposure lands on the person rather than the institution.

How outcomes are evaluated

In a highly contained environment, evaluation criteria exist in advance. You know what reliable performance looks like before the mission starts. In a less contained environment, evaluation is often retrospective—defined by outcomes after the fact, interpreted through relationships and organizational context, and rarely tied to standards that were established before the work began.

These four conditions—authority, roles, risk, and evaluation—are the structural signals you will learn to read in every environment you enter. Together, they tell you what kind of system you are actually dealing with before you invest time, effort, and career decisions into it.

◆ ◆ ◆

The Three Tiers

Civilian environments fall across a spectrum of structural containment. That spectrum can be organized into three broad conditions (not rigid boxes but recognizable patterns that show up consistently enough to be useful as a classification tool).

Tier 1 — Bounded

Tier 1 environments are the most structurally contained civilian systems that exist. Authority is explicit and traceable. Roles are predefined and documented. Evaluation criteria exist in advance. The institution absorbs significant risk on behalf of the people operating inside it.

Large federal agencies are the clearest example. Position classifications exist before the hire. Performance standards are documented. Authority chains are codified in regulation. The institution has been designed, sometimes over decades, to function independently of any individual inside it.

Large established corporations with formal governance structures occupy this tier as well. So do highly regulated industries—healthcare systems, financial institutions, defense contractors operating under federal contract requirements—where external oversight creates structural containment even when internal management does not.

Veterans entering Tier 1 environments often feel the most immediate sense of familiarity. The signals are recognizable. Authority is traceable. Expectations exist in advance. The feedback mechanisms, while different from the military's, operate on a more defined rhythm than what most civilian environments provide.

Tier 1 is not identical to the military. It is the closest civilian approximation of the structural conditions veterans were trained in. The gap still exists—and it still matters—but it is a narrower gap than what veterans encounter in most other civilian environments.

Tier 2 — Unbounded

Tier 2 environments have structure, but it is incomplete, inconsistently applied, or unevenly distributed across the organization. Authority exists but moves through informal channels as often as formal ones. Roles are defined but shift based on organizational need, personnel changes, and evolving priorities. Evaluation happens, but the criteria are not always established in advance. Risk is partially absorbed by the institution and partially carried by individuals.

Most mid-sized civilian organizations operate in Tier 2. These include: small businesses that have grown past their founding stage but have not yet built formal governance systems; many nonprofits; and many private firms that operate in competitive markets where structural formality has been traded for speed and flexibility.

Tier 2 is where many veterans land. It is also where most of the friction described in Chapter 2 originates. Because Tier 2 environments have enough structure to look organized from the outside but not enough consistency to behave predictably from the inside. Authority looks clear until a decision needs to be made, and suddenly, three people have overlapping ownership. Roles look defined until the person who defined them leaves. Evaluation looks formal until review time comes and the criteria turn out to be largely subjective.

Tier 2 is not a broken system. It is a system operating under constraints—resource constraints, speed constraints, market constraints—that make full structural containment difficult to maintain. Understanding that is what allows a veteran to operate effectively inside it rather than spending energy trying to turn it into something it was never designed to be.

Tier 3 — The Nothing

Tier 3 is not a poorly structured organization. It is the absence of organizational structure entirely.

In Tier 3, there is no stable authority. No predefined roles. No evaluation framework that exists in advance. No institutional risk absorption. Effort goes in, and the connection between that effort and any outcome is direct, unmediated, and entirely personal. When something goes wrong in Tier 3, there is no system to catch it. When something goes right, there is no system to build on it.

Early-stage entrepreneurship is the clearest example of Tier 3. So is gig work, informal self-employment, and any situation where a veteran is operating without an organizational structure underneath them. The Nothing is not defined by industry or income level. It is defined by the absence of the structural conditions that make effort accumulate.

Veterans enter Tier 3 more often than any other group, and with less preparation for what they are walking into. The appeal is real: ownership, autonomy, the ability to build something without the constraints of an institution. What is rarely explained is that those institutional constraints were also doing something valuable. They were absorbing risk. They were providing evaluation criteria. They were building continuity. In Tier 3, all of that disappears, and the veteran is left holding everything the institution used to carry.

Tier 3 is not a death sentence. Many veterans have built successful businesses starting from nothing. But they did it by understanding what they were dealing with and by building the structural conditions that Tier 3 does not provide on its own. That process is examined in detail in Volume III. For now, the critical thing is being able to recognize when you are in Tier 3 before you have committed considerable time, resources, and personal exposure to it.

What Comes Next

The tier definitions give you the vocabulary. The next chapter shows you what each tier looks like from the inside through specific situations, observable signals, and a consistent reference point, so the structural differences become visible in practice, not just in theory.

The three-tier framework draws on documented patterns in organizational structure research and veteran transition literature. Tier classifications reflect consistent structural differences observable across organizational types, not prescriptive categories. Individual organizations may exhibit characteristics of more than one tier simultaneously or shift tier position over time as governance structures evolve.

CHAPTER 4

THE THREE TIERS IN PRACTICE

The tier framework is not a judgment system. It does not tell you that Tier 1 is good and Tier 3 is bad. It does not tell you where to work or what to build. What it gives you is a way to read the structural conditions of any environment before you commit to operating inside it so that effort goes into environments you understand, not environments you are still trying to decode.

Key Terms

Tier position: Where an organization sits on the structural containment spectrum at a given point in time. Tier position can shift as organizations grow, lose governance, or change operating conditions.

The spectrum: The full range of structural containment from fully bounded (Tier 1) to completely unstructured (Tier 3). Most organizations sit between the markers rather than at the extremes.

The tier definitions in chapter 3 describe structural conditions in the abstract. This chapter shows what those conditions look like from the inside—through Taylor, through observable signals, and through the spectrum that connects all three tiers into a single readable framework.

The Spectrum, Not the Box

The three tiers are not rigid categories. They are positions on a spectrum of structural containment that runs from fully bounded at one end to completely unstructured at the other.

Most real organizations sit somewhere between the markers. A Tier 2 organization with strong financial controls and a well-defined authority structure might operate closer to Tier 1 in some functions and closer to Tier 3 in others. A federal contractor might be firmly Tier 1 under contract requirements but slide toward Tier 2 in how it manages internal operations where those requirements do not apply.

The spectrum also moves. Organizations change their tier position over time. A startup that builds governance architecture moves from Tier 3 toward Tier 2. A large corporation that loses key structure through rapid growth, leadership turnover, or market disruption can slide from Tier 1 toward Tier 2. The classification you make today is accurate for today, which is why the diagnostic method introduced later includes a re-evaluation step.

What matters is not placing every organization into a perfect box. What matters is developing the ability to read where an organization sits on the spectrum—accurately enough to understand what it can and cannot provide before you make decisions that depend on it.

◆ ◆ ◆

Taylor Across Three Tiers

Taylor is a project manager. The branch does not matter. The years of service do not matter. What matters is that Taylor performs consistently across all three environments below. The competence does not change. The effort does not change. The outcomes do.

Taylor in Tier 1

Taylor takes a project management role at a federal agency. The position existed before Taylor applied—documented, classified, with established performance standards. On the first day, there is a structured onboarding. The authority chain is clear. Taylor's role connects to other roles through documented processes. Feedback comes through a formal review cycle tied to standards that were defined in advance.

Six months in, Taylor is performing well. The environment is not identical to the military. The pace is different, the mission is different, the culture is different. But the structural signals are readable. Authority is traceable. Expectations were defined before the work started. Taylor knows how performance will be evaluated before the evaluation happens.

The gap still exists. But Taylor can navigate it.

Taylor in Tier 2

Taylor takes a project management role at a mid-sized technology firm. The role was described clearly in the job posting. The first week is less structured than expected: Onboarding is informal, the role boundaries turn out to be broader and less defined than the posting suggested, and the authority structure that looked clear on the organizational chart turns out to operate differently in practice.

Six months in, Taylor is working hard and producing results. But the results are not being read consistently. A project that Taylor managed exceptionally well receives little recognition because the person who would have recognized it left the company in month three. A process Taylor built to improve team coordination gets quietly dismantled by a manager who prefers the informal approach. Feedback comes irregularly, and when it does come, it is tied to criteria Taylor was not given in advance.

Taylor is not failing. Taylor is operating in a Tier 2 environment: one with enough structure to look organized but not enough consistency to behave predictably. Understanding that does not fix the environment. But it stops Taylor from interpreting the inconsistency as personal failure, and it informs the decision about whether to stay, adapt, or move.

Taylor in Tier 3

Taylor leaves the technology firm and starts a consulting practice. The work is real. The clients come. The revenue arrives. For the first several months, everything feels like progress.

Then a key client leaves. The revenue that felt stable turns out to have been concentrated in one relationship. There is no process for replacing it because there was never a process for generating it. It came through a personal connection and left the same way. Taylor works harder. Takes on more. Fills every hour with activity.

And the activity does not accumulate the way it did inside an organization.

In Tier 3, there is no institutional structure to build on. Every client relationship is personal. Every process lives in Taylor's head. Every risk lands directly on Taylor with nothing underneath to absorb it. The effort is real. The capability is real. The structure that used to convert effort into accumulated outcomes is gone.

Taylor is not failing. Taylor is in The Nothing and doing what most people do when they first get there, which is applying the logic of an organizational system to conditions where no organizational system exists. Recognizing that is the first step toward building one.

◆ ◆ ◆

What This Framework Gives You

The tier framework gives you a way to read the structural conditions of any environment before you commit to operating inside it. A Tier 1 environment offers containment and predictability but may move slowly and reward conformity over initiative. A Tier 2 environment offers flexibility and opportunity but requires the ability to operate effectively without consistent structural support. A Tier 3 environment offers complete autonomy but requires building the structural conditions that other tiers provide automatically.

None of those is universally better than the others. What matters is knowing which one you are in and whether it matches what you need, what you are prepared for, and what you are trying to build.

That is what the framework gives you. Not an answer. A way to read the question accurately.

What Comes Next

The tier framework classifies environments at the macro level. But veterans do not experience organizations at the macro level; they experience them through specific situations. A job interview. The first week of onboarding. A meeting where a decision does not get made. An email that goes unanswered for two weeks.

The next chapter narrows the lens from the organization to the situation and shows how to read the structural signals that appear in individual interactions before the larger pattern becomes visible.

Tier position is observable through structural signals, not organizational claims. An organization's self-description—in job postings, mission statements, or onboarding materials—frequently reflects aspirational rather than actual structural conditions. The diagnostic method in Chapter 9 addresses this gap directly.

PART THREE

Reading Situations

CHAPTER 5

THE SMALL PICTURE: HOW SYSTEMS ARE LIVED THROUGH SITUATIONS

◆ ◆ ◆

Veterans do not experience organizations as systems; they experience them as situations. A conversation, a meeting, an email, a first week. The error is in interpreting those situations as personal signals when they are structural ones. This chapter teaches the difference and introduces the four high-signal situations where structural misattribution is most likely to occur.

◆ ◆ ◆

Key Terms

Structural misattribution: The act of interpreting a system-produced outcome as a personal one. The most common and most costly error veterans make when reading civilian environments.

Structural literacy: The ability to pause in a specific situation and ask whether an outcome was produced by personal performance or by the structural conditions of the environment.

Surface content: The first layer of a situation—what was said, what happened, what the outcome was.

Structural signal: The second layer of a situation—what the outcome reveals about how authority, roles, risk, and evaluation actually operate in that environment.

◆ ◆ ◆

You do not walk into an organization.

You walk into a Monday morning. A first meeting. An email that does not get answered. A conversation where the decision you expected to be made gets deferred to someone who was not in the room.

You walk into situations. And those situations—not the organizational chart, not the mission statement, not the onboarding packet—are how the system actually reveals itself to you.

Chapter 3 gave you the framework for reading organizations at the macro level. The three tiers. The structural containment spectrum. The four observable conditions that tell you what kind of system you are dealing with. That framework is real, and it is useful. You cannot confirm a tier from the outside. You can read early signals—and later volumes will show you how—but the system reveals itself fully through specific moments. You experience it through specific encounters, and those moments arrive one at a time, often before you have any sense of the larger picture.

This chapter narrows the lens from the organization to the situation. From the macro system to the moment you are actually standing in.

And it addresses the most common and most costly error veterans make when they get there.

◆ ◆ ◆

The Core Error: Structural Misattribution

Structural misattribution is the act of interpreting a system-produced outcome as a personal one.

It happens when a veteran goes through a full interview process for a role the organization has already decided to fill internally and concludes they were not good enough, even though the outcome was never actually in play. When a process they built gets quietly dismantled, they conclude that they misread the organization's needs. When a decision they expected to be made gets deferred indefinitely, they conclude that they failed to advocate effectively. When feedback never arrives, they conclude that their performance was not strong enough to warrant it.

In each case, the interpretation is personal. The cause is structural.

The interview was not a genuine evaluation; it was a compliance process for a role that had already been filled internally. The process was dismantled because the organization lacks the structural continuity to sustain initiatives beyond the person who launched them. The decision was deferred because authority in that organization operates informally, and the person with actual decision-making power was not present. The feedback did not arrive because there is no feedback mechanism, not because the performance did not merit one.

None of that has anything to do with the veteran's capability, preparation, or judgment.

But structural misattribution turns it into evidence of personal failure, and that misreading compounds over time. The veteran adjusts their approach. Works harder. Changes their communication style. Recalibrates their expectations. And nothing improves, because the source of the problem was never personal to begin with.

The antidote is not optimism. It is not resilience training or a better mindset. It is structural literacy: the ability to pause in a specific situation and ask the right question before drawing a conclusion.

Is this about me—or about the system I am in?

What a Situation Actually Contains

Many situations a veteran encounters during transition contain two layers of information.

The first layer is the surface content—what was said, what happened, what the outcome was. The interview went well, but no offer came. The manager praised the work, but the promotion did not follow. The onboarding was enthusiastic, but the role was never clearly defined.

The second layer is the structural signal—what the situation reveals about how authority, roles, risk, and evaluation actually operate in that environment.

Most people read the first layer and stop there. The interview did not produce an offer, so the interview must have fallen short. The promotion did not follow the praise, so the praise must have been empty. The role was never defined, so the manager must have been disorganized.

Those readings are not always wrong. Sometimes the interview did fall short. Sometimes the manager is disorganized. But in a large number of cases—particularly in Tier 2 and Tier 3 environments—the surface outcome is produced by structural conditions that have nothing to do with the individual at the center of it.

Learning to read the second layer does not mean ignoring the first. It means holding both and not collapsing the structural signal into a personal one before you have enough information to know which layer produced the outcome.

◆ ◆ ◆

Situations Veterans Encounter Most

Transition surfaces a predictable set of situations where structural misattribution is most likely to occur. Each one contains structural signals that are readable once you know what to look for.

The interview

What it looks like on the surface: a mutual evaluation. The organization assesses the candidate. The candidate assesses the organization. Both sides.

What it often is structurally: a process whose relationship to an actual hiring decision varies significantly by tier.

In a Tier 1 environment, the interview is usually a genuine evaluation. The role exists, the criteria are predefined, and the process is designed to produce a decision. Feedback—formal or informal—often follows. You can read the interview as a real signal about fit.

In a Tier 2 environment, the interview is less predictable. The role may be loosely defined. The evaluation criteria may not have been established before the process began. The hiring decision may depend on relationships and informal dynamics that the interview itself does not surface. An interview that felt strong can produce no offer because the decision is made through channels the interview did not access.

In a Tier 3 environment—early-stage businesses, informal arrangements, entrepreneurial ventures—the interview may be nearly indistinguishable from a conversation. There is often no formal process, no predefined criteria, and no institutional mechanism that converts the conversation into a decision. The outcome depends almost entirely on personal dynamics and immediate fit. That is not a flaw in how you interviewed. It is a structural condition of the environment.

The signal to read: How structured was the process? Were the criteria defined in advance, or did the conversation feel like it was defining them in real time? Was there a clear authority figure who owned the decision, or did it feel like the answer would emerge from somewhere you could not quite locate?

The first ninety days

What it looks like on the surface: an orientation period. A chance to learn the organization, demonstrate value, and establish yourself in the role.

What it often is structurally: the period in which the actual structural conditions of the organization become visible for the first time.

In a Tier 1 environment, the first ninety days tend to be structured. Onboarding exists. The role is defined. Expectations are communicated—sometimes formally, sometimes through established practice. You may feel friction, but the structural signals are readable. You know what you are doing, who you report to, and how your performance will be evaluated.

In a Tier 2 environment, the first ninety days often feel like the organization is figuring out what to do with you at the same time you are figuring out what you are supposed to be doing. The role that was described in the interview turns out to be broader, narrower, or different in ways that were not communicated in advance. Authority turns out to operate differently from what the organizational chart suggested. The person who hired you may not be the person who most influences your work. Onboarding may be informal, incomplete, or absent.

None of that is a signal about your performance. It is a signal about the structural containment of the environment. A Tier 2 organization does not have a poorly run onboarding because its HR department is incompetent. It has a variable onboarding because it does not have the structural consistency to deliver a standardized one. That is a different diagnosis, and it calls for a different response.

In a Tier 3 environment, the first ninety days may feel like building the job from scratch while also doing the job. There is no onboarding because there is no structure that would produce one. Expectations are implicit, evolving, and often never stated directly. The feedback loop that would tell you how you are doing does not yet exist. That is not a management failure. It is Tier 3.

The signal to read: Was onboarding structured or improvised? Were expectations stated before you started or discovered through the work? Did the role you were hired into match the role you found yourself doing? The gap between what was described and what you encountered is structural data.

The decision that does not get made

A meeting ends without a decision. An email asking for direction goes unanswered for two weeks. A project stalls while waiting for approval that never arrives. A question about priorities produces a conversation instead of an answer.

The natural interpretation: Something went wrong. The wrong people were in the room. The request was not framed clearly. The relationship with the decision-maker needs work.

The structural interpretation: The decision-making authority in this organization is not where the organizational chart says it is.

In Tier 1 environments, decision authority is typically explicit. You may not always agree with the decision, and the process may move slowly, but you can usually trace where the decision lives and what it will take to get one. The machinery exists.

In Tier 2 environments, decision authority is one of the most variable structural conditions. Formal authority and actual authority frequently diverge. The person with the title may not be the person with the influence. Decisions that appear to belong to one level of the organization may actually require consensus from people who are not formally part of the process. A meeting that should produce a decision produces a conversation instead, not because the participants were confused, but because real decision authority was not in the room.

This is not a communication problem. It is an authority problem. And the way to address it is not to communicate better with the same people. It is to read the authority structure more accurately and find where the real decision actually lies.

The signal to read: Who was in the room when a decision needed to be made? Was the decision made or deferred? If deferred, to whom and on what basis? The pattern of deferred decisions tells you where authority actually sits in the organization.

Feedback that does not arrive

You complete a significant piece of work. You wait for feedback. Nothing comes. You follow up. You receive a vague positive response that does not address the substance of what you did. Or nothing at all.

The natural interpretation: The work was not strong enough to merit a response. The manager is avoiding a difficult conversation. Your performance is not where it needs to be.

The structural interpretation: The feedback mechanism may not exist.

Military service operates inside one of the most codified performance evaluation systems in any organizational context. Evaluation criteria are defined in advance. Review cycles are structured. Feedback is institutionalized: It arrives whether or not it is comfortable to deliver.

Most civilian organizations—particularly in Tier 2 and Tier 3—do not have that. Feedback in those environments is often informal, irregular, and heavily dependent on the individual manager's willingness and capacity to deliver it. Some managers are skilled at it. Many are not. Some organizations have formal review processes that function well. Many have formal processes that exist on paper and do not function as designed. Some have no structured feedback mechanism at all.

When feedback does not arrive, the absence is information: It is information about the structural feedback environment, not about the quality of the work. The two can be related. They are frequently not.

The signal to read: Is there a formal feedback mechanism, and does it actually function? Has feedback arrived consistently for others in comparable roles? Is the absence of feedback specific to you, or is it the default condition of the environment? The answer tells you what the absence means.

◆ ◆ ◆

What Comes Next

Each of the four situations above carries structural signals that become readable once the habit of asking the right question is installed. The next chapter shows that habit in action—through Taylor, across three situations, in three different structural environments. The concept becomes visible through the application.

Structural misattribution is documented in veteran transition research as one of the most persistent sources of post-separation friction. When veterans attribute system-produced outcomes to personal performance, the result is self-corrective behavior applied to conditions that individual behavior did not cause and cannot fix.

The four high-signal situations described in this chapter reflect consistent patterns across veteran transition accounts and organizational behavior research.

CHAPTER 6

READING THE SIGNAL: TAYLOR ACROSS THREE SITUATIONS

◆ ◆ ◆

Structural literacy is not a concept to understand once and set aside. It is a habit to install, one question to ask before drawing a conclusion from any outcome that feels personal. This chapter shows that habit in action through three Taylor scenarios, each in a different structural environment and each producing an outcome that structural misattribution would turn into a false verdict on performance.

◆ ◆ ◆

Key Terms

The diagnostic question: "Is this about me—or about the system I am in?" The habit that converts structural literacy from a concept into a practice.

Compliance process: A hiring or evaluation process conducted to satisfy procedural requirements rather than to produce a genuine selection. Common in Tier 2 organizations filling roles with internal candidates.

◆ ◆ ◆

The four situations in chapter 5 carry structural signals that become readable once the habit is installed. This chapter shows the habit in action—Taylor, three situations, three different structural environments.

◆ ◆ ◆

Taylor Across Three Situations

Taylor is a logistics and operations specialist. The branch does not matter. The years of service do not matter. In each scenario below, Taylor encounters the same type of situation in a different structural environment. The competence does not change. The effort does not change. The outcomes do.

Taylor and the job that was not really open

Taylor applies for an operations manager role at a mid-sized distribution company. The job posting is detailed. The interview process involves three rounds: a phone screen, a panel interview, and a final conversation with the VP of operations. Taylor prepares thoroughly, and the interviews go well. The VP tells Taylor the panel was impressed. Two weeks later, a formal rejection arrives.

Taylor's first interpretation: Something in the final interview did not land. Maybe the salary expectation was off. Maybe there was a stronger candidate. Maybe the questions about process improvement signaled something negative.

What the structural picture shows: The company had a strong internal candidate for the role—a team lead who had been in the organization for four years. The external search was launched to satisfy an HR requirement that open positions be posted publicly before an internal promotion is finalized. Three rounds of interviews were conducted. The outcome was determined before the first call was scheduled.

Taylor did not fail the interview. Taylor participated in a process whose purpose was compliance, not selection. The rejection was not a signal about Taylor's readiness. It was a signal about how that organization fills roles.

The question Taylor should be asking is not what went wrong in the interview. It is "What does this tell me about how this organization's hiring actually works, and do I want to pursue roles here again?"

Taylor and the feedback that never came

Taylor joins a nonprofit as a program coordinator. The role involves managing a portfolio of community programs, coordinating with partner organizations, and reporting on outcomes to funders. Taylor takes the work seriously, builds relationships with partners, delivers reports on time, and improves several processes that were producing errors in the previous cycle.

After six months, Taylor has received no formal feedback. A mid-year check-in was scheduled and then canceled twice. When Taylor asks the director directly how things are going, the response is warm but vague—"You're doing great, keep it up"—with no reference to the specific work Taylor has been doing.

Taylor's first interpretation: The lack of specificity means something is being withheld. The director is managing around a problem rather than naming it. Performance must be acceptable but not strong.

What the structural picture shows: The organization has a written performance review process that the director is aware of and has not prioritized. The director manages five coordinators and spends most of their capacity on funder relationships and board management. Feedback in this organization has always been informal and irregular, not because performance is irrelevant but because there is no structural mechanism that makes feedback delivery a consistent organizational output. The director's vague response is not concealment. It is the default mode of a Tier 2 feedback environment.

Taylor is performing well. The absence of feedback is not evidence to the contrary. It is evidence about the structural feedback conditions of the environment, and it is the same evidence that every coordinator in that organization has been receiving for years.

Taylor and the authority that moved

Taylor is eight months into a role at a growing technology company. A project Taylor has been leading is ready for a key decision: which of two vendor platforms to move forward with. Taylor has done the analysis, built the comparison, and presented the recommendation to the direct manager, who agrees and tells Taylor to move forward.

Two weeks later, nothing has moved. Taylor follows up. The manager says they are still working through the decision. Another two weeks pass. Taylor learns through a colleague that the company's COO—who was not part of any prior conversation about the project —has questions about the vendor selection and that the project is effectively on hold until those questions are addressed.

Taylor's first interpretation: The manager overpromised authority they did not have. The project was handled incorrectly. A different escalation path should have been used from the start.

What the structural picture shows: In this organization, decisions involving vendor contracts above a certain value require COO sign-off, but that threshold is not documented anywhere. It is known informally by people who have navigated it before and is unknown to people who have not. Taylor's manager had authority to approve the direction but not the contract. The gap between those two things was invisible until the decision tried to move through it.

This is not a failure of process management. It is a Tier 2 authority structure behaving exactly as Tier 2 authority structures behave: visible at the surface, inconsistent underneath. The question Taylor should be asking is not what should have been done differently. It is "What does this tell me about where authority actually lives in decisions of this type, and how do I map that before the next one?"

Installing the Habit

Structural literacy is not a concept to understand. It is a habit to install.

The habit is simple. It is not easy. Every time a situation produces an outcome that feels like a personal signal—a rejection, a stalled decision, absent feedback, a role that turned out differently than described—the habit asks one question before drawing a conclusion:

Is this about me—or about the system I am in?

That question does not replace accountability. If the interview fell short because of preparation, the habit will surface that. If the performance actually was not strong enough, the habit will surface that too. The question is not a way of deflecting responsibility. It is a way of ensuring that the diagnosis is accurate before any response is built on top of it.

The military trained you to debrief. To distinguish what the environment produced from what the operator produced. To ask what conditions were fixed and what conditions were under your control. This is the same discipline applied to a different terrain.

You are not starting from zero. You are applying an existing analytical habit to a new context—one where the structural conditions are less visible, the signals are less codified, and the defaults will push you toward personal explanation before structural ones.

The framework gives you the vocabulary to resist that pull. The habit is what makes the vocabulary useful.

◆ ◆ ◆

What Comes Next

The tier framework classifies environments at the macro level. This chapter has shown how to read structural signals at the situational level—in the specific moments where systems become visible through outcomes.

But one tier requires its own chapter. Tier 3—The Nothing—is not simply the low end of a spectrum. It is a structurally distinct condition that produces specific patterns of friction that cannot be read through the same lens as Tier 1 or Tier 2. Veterans enter it more often than any other group. They are less prepared for what they find there than in any other environment.

The next chapter examines The Nothing directly—what it is, what it is not, what it does to effort and identity over time, and how to recognize it before you have invested too much inside it.

The three Taylor scenarios in this chapter are composites drawn from patterns that appear consistently in veteran transition accounts. Names, organizations, and identifying details are fictional. The structural conditions each scenario illustrates— compliance hiring processes, absent feedback mechanisms, and informal authority thresholds—are documented features of Tier 2 organizational environments.

PART FOUR

The Nothing

Chapter 7

The Nothing: When There Is No System at All

◆ ◆ ◆

Tier 3—The Nothing—is not a weak or poorly run organization. It is the complete absence of organizational structure. Veterans enter it in two ways: by choosing it through entrepreneurship or self-employment and by being hired into it without knowing it was there. This chapter names what The Nothing is, what distinguishes it from Tier 2, and why both paths into it lead to the same structural conditions.

◆ ◆ ◆

Key Terms

The Nothing (Tier 3): The complete absence of organizational structure. No stable authority, predefined roles, advanced evaluation criteria, or institutional risk absorption. Tier 3 is distinct from Tier 2, which has an incomplete structure. By contrast, Tier 3 has none.

The chosen path: Entry into Tier 3 through deliberate choice—entrepreneurship, consulting, or self-employment. The absence of institutional constraint is part of the appeal.

The accidental path: Entry into Tier 3 through a hiring process that presented the organization as more structured than it actually was. The veteran arrives expecting Tier 2 and finds Tier 3.

Institutional floor: The baseline of structural support that military service always provided—risk absorption, evaluation framework, authority continuity—even in austere operating environments. Tier 3 has no equivalent.

◆ ◆ ◆

There are two ways to end up in The Nothing: by choice or by accident. The first is deliberate, encompassing entrepreneurship, consulting, or self-employment, where veterans trade institutional structure for autonomy and keep what they build. The second is unintentionally, where a role that looked organized from the outside turns out to have no defined structure, no onboarding, and no clear authority once you arrive. The organization presented as a Tier 2; the interior is something closer to Tier 3.

Both paths lead to the same place. And the description of that place is the same regardless of how you got there.

What it leaves out (in both cases) is everything the institution was doing that you never had to think about because the institution was doing it. The risk absorption. The evaluation framework. The continuity that allowed effort to accumulate from one week to the next. The structural conditions that converted individual capability into organizational outcomes.

In Tier 3, all of that is gone. Not reduced. Not inconsistent. Gone.

That is what this chapter is about.

◆ ◆ ◆

What The Nothing Actually Is

The Nothing is not a poorly structured organization. It is not a startup that has not hired an HR director yet, or a small business that runs lean, or a nonprofit that trades formality for mission focus. Those are Tier 2: organizations with incomplete or uneven structure but structure nonetheless.

The Nothing is the complete absence of organizational structure. No stable authority. No predefined roles. No evaluation framework that exists in advance. No institutional mechanism to absorb risk on behalf of the people operating inside it.

The distinction matters because the response is different. A Tier 2 organization with a weak structure can often be navigated. You can find where authority actually lives, build informal evaluation criteria, and identify who absorbs risk and how. The structural conditions are incomplete, but they exist. You can work with them.

In The Nothing, there is nothing to find. There is no hidden authority structure. There are no informal evaluation criteria operating beneath the formal ones. There are no criteria at all. Every process, every standard, every structure that would allow effort to accumulate into something durable has to be built from scratch. By you. While you are also doing the work.

That is true whether you are the founder of the organization or its newest hire. The Nothing does not change its character based on who is standing inside it. A veteran hired into a founder-led startup with no documented processes, no defined authority structure, and no institutional risk absorption is in Tier 3, regardless of the job title on the offer letter.

That is not a management problem. It is a structural condition. And it calls for a completely different orientation than anything the military—or most civilian employment—prepared you for.

Why Veterans End Up There

As mentioned, veterans enter Tier 3 more often than any other group. They arrive through two distinct paths, and both are worth understanding.

The chosen path

The first reason veterans choose Tier 3 is the appeal of ownership. After years inside a system where nearly every parameter of professional life was defined externally (what you wore, where you lived, what you did, how you were evaluated), the prospect of building something entirely your own carries genuine weight. Autonomy is not a small thing after a career spent with very little of it.

The second reason is the skills match. Veterans leave service with capabilities that translate directly into entrepreneurial contexts (logistics, operations, leadership under pressure, decision-making with incomplete information, the ability to execute without supervision). Those competencies are real. The people encouraging veterans toward entrepreneurship are not wrong that the skills exist.

The third reason is the transition gap itself. Many veterans separate without a clear employment path. The civilian job market does not always recognize military experience in ways that produce immediate opportunities. Entrepreneurship fills that gap, and it fills it with something that feels like agency rather than waiting.

The accidental path

The fourth reason veterans end up in Tier 3 is that they did not know they were entering it.

Early-stage companies, founder-led organizations, and rapidly growing small businesses frequently present as structured from the outside. The job posting is detailed. The interview involves multiple people. The offer is formal. Nothing in the process signals that the organizational infrastructure described during recruiting does not yet exist or exists only on paper.

The veteran accepts the role in good faith. The first week reveals a different reality. Onboarding is improvised or absent. The role described in the interview is broader, less defined, or simply different from what was advertised. The authority structure that appeared on the organizational chart turns out to be aspirational rather than operational. Processes that were referenced during the interview process have not been built.

This is not deception in most cases. The people who hired the veteran often genuinely believe their organization is more structured than it is. Founders in particular frequently cannot see the gap between the organization they are describing and the organization that actually exists because they are inside it, and inside The Nothing, the absence of structure can feel like flexibility rather than absence.

The veteran who arrives expecting Tier 2 and finds Tier 3 faces a specific version of structural misattribution: They begin adjusting their own behavior to compensate for structural conditions they have not yet named. They work harder. They build processes informally. They absorb the risk that the organization was supposed to carry. And they interpret the friction as a sign that they are still finding their footing rather than a sign that the footing was never built.

What Military Training Does Not Prepare You For

This is not a criticism of military training. It is a structural observation.

Military service is Tier 1 in its most complete form. Authority is explicit. Roles are predefined. Evaluation criteria are codified. Risk is absorbed institutionally. The system is designed to function regardless of the individual inside it and to produce consistent outcomes across a vast range of people, contexts, and operational conditions.

Many veterans did build systems in uniform. They were senior NCOs who constructed training programs from nothing. Officers who stood up new commands or operated in austere environments where the institutional playbook did not exist. Veterans who led small teams far from the support structure of a large installation and had to create what they needed on the ground.

That experience is real. What is also true is that even in those cases, the institutional floor was still there. The military was still absorbing a baseline of risk. Evaluation still existed within a codified framework, even when the specific criteria had to be adapted. Authority still traced back through a chain that had been established before the mission began.

The task in Tier 3 is different: not just building but building without that floor underneath you. No institutional risk absorption to fall back on. No evaluation framework that existed before you arrived. No authority structure that predates your presence. Whatever structural conditions the environment needs, you are responsible for constructing them while also doing the work they are supposed to support.

That gap applies equally to the veteran who chooses Tier 3 and the veteran who is hired into it. The chosen path and the accidental path land in the same place: operating inside a system that does not exist yet, without the institutional floor that military service—even at its most austere—always provided.

◆ ◆ ◆

What Comes Next

Knowing what The Nothing is and how you get there is the first half of the picture. The second half is what The Nothing does over time: the pattern of early momentum followed by the fractures, the erosion of structural feedback, and the signals that make it recognizable once you are inside it. That is what the next chapter covers.

Among the veterans examined in this research, early-stage entrepreneurship appeared at a notably high rate, often not by choice but as a response to structural conditions that left few other viable paths. The pattern included both the appeal of ownership following structured service and elevated risk of business failure in the absence of structural preparation. The Nothing is not a critique of entrepreneurial choice; it is a structural description of the conditions that make that choice more complex than it is typically presented.

CHAPTER 8

WHAT THE NOTHING DOES: PATTERN, RECOGNITION, AND NAVIGATION

The Nothing follows a consistent pattern: early momentum, a fracture through concentration, an effort response that addresses the wrong problem, and an erosion of the structural feedback that told you whether work was building toward something. This chapter describes that pattern, names the signals that make Tier 3 recognizable from inside it, and closes with what the framework actually gives you: not avoidance of hard terrain but accurate navigation of it.

Key Terms

Concentration risk: The condition in which revenue, relationships, or institutional knowledge is held in a sole source. The first fracture in The Nothing typically arrives through concentration—when that single source moves.

Structural feedback: The institutional signals that tell an operator whether effort is building toward something durable. Performance cycles, promotion boards, evaluation criteria. Tier 3 has none of these by default.

Role-person fusion: The condition in which no boundary exists between the work and the individual doing it. Everything depends on one person specifically; nothing functions without that person specifically. A primary signal of Tier 3.

Chapter 7 described what The Nothing is and how veterans arrive there, by choice and by accident. This chapter describes what happens next: the consistent pattern that follows entry, the signals that make Tier 3 recognizable from inside it, and what the framework actually equips you to do once you have named where you are.

◆ ◆ ◆

What The Nothing Does Over Time

The pattern is consistent enough to describe, and it looks the same whether the veteran built the organization or was hired into it.

In the preliminary period, The Nothing feels like momentum. There is activity. Clients come, or revenue arrives, or projects launch. The absence of institutional constraint feels like speed. In the chosen path, you are not waiting for approvals. In the accidental path, the energy of a growing organization feels like forward motion. Either way, something is happening.

The first fracture usually arrives through concentration. A key client leaves. A primary revenue source dries up. A founding team member departs and takes undocumented institutional knowledge with them. What felt like a diversified foundation turns out to have been a single relationship or a single source, and when it goes, it takes a disproportionate share of the structure with it.

The response is effort. More hours. More outreach. More activity. This is the natural response, and it addresses the wrong problem, not because effort is wrong but because effort in The Nothing does not accumulate the way it does inside a structured organization. In a structured environment, effort builds on itself. Processes retain the work. Systems carry the output forward. In The Nothing, each effort largely stands alone. The wheel turns, but nothing is stored.

The second fracture is identity. Veterans who built their professional identity inside the most structured system in modern society often find that identity eroding in The Nothing, not because they are performing poorly but because the feedback mechanisms that told them what superior performance looked like are gone. There is no evaluation cycle. No promotion board. No formal recognition. No institutional signal that the work matters or that the direction is right.

Over time, the absence of structural feedback makes it difficult to distinguish between a period of challenging work that is building toward something and a period of hard work that is simply being absorbed by the void. That distinction—which any structured environment would make visible—is invisible in Tier 3 until the financial or organizational consequences make it undeniable.

None of this is inevitable. But it is the predictable pattern of The Nothing when entered without structural awareness and without a deliberate effort to build what it does not provide.

How to Recognize It

The Nothing is recognizable before you commit to it, and once you are already inside it. The signals are the same regardless of which path brought you there.

The clearest signal is the absence of an evaluation framework. Ask "How will anyone know, six months from now, whether this is working?" If the answer is revenue alone, or activity alone, or founder enthusiasm alone, you are looking at a Tier 3 environment. Those are real measures. They are not structural ones. An organization that evaluates itself only through output has no mechanism for distinguishing between output that is building something durable and output that is masking structural fragility.

The second signal is role definition. In The Nothing, roles do not exist before the person creates them, whether that person is a founder building a business or a new hire trying to understand what they were actually brought in to do. The absence of role definition is not a problem in itself. It becomes a problem when there is no boundary between the work and the person doing it—when everything depends on one individual specifically, and nothing functions without that individual specifically.

The third signal is risk location. In every structured environment, some portion of risk is absorbed by the institution. In The Nothing, all of it lands on the individual. Every client relationship is personal. Every process lives in someone's head. Every financial or operational exposure is carried without an institutional buffer. For the veteran who chose this path, that exposure was part of the decision. For the veteran who was hired into it, that exposure may never have been disclosed because the organization may not have recognized it was there.

If you are reading these signals and recognizing where you are, that recognition is the starting point. Not a reason for alarm. A structural diagnosis, which is exactly what this book has been building toward.

◆ ◆ ◆

Taylor in The Nothing — Two Versions

Taylor is a logistics and operations specialist. The branch does not matter. The years of service do not matter. Below are two versions of Taylor in Tier 3: one who chose it and one who was hired into it without knowing.

Taylor who built it

Taylor separates and launches a consulting practice. Former colleagues become first clients. Within three months, two contracts are running. The revenue is real. The work is familiar. The absence of institutional friction feels like clarity.

Six months in, one contract ends. The client's budget was cut; nothing Taylor did or did not do. The remaining contract covers about sixty percent of what Taylor needs. Taylor works harder. Takes on smaller projects to fill the gap. Spends evenings on outreach that produces conversations but not contracts.

A year in, Taylor is working more hours than at any point in uniform. The revenue is roughly equivalent to what Taylor earned before separating. But there is no path visible from where Taylor is standing. No evaluation framework to indicate whether the business is building toward something or simply sustaining. Every client relationship lives entirely in Taylor's direct involvement. Nothing works without Taylor in it.

Taylor is not failing. Taylor is in The Nothing and has been applying the logic of an organizational system to conditions where no organizational system exists. The first step is the same one this book has been building toward: accurate classification. Taylor is in Tier 3. That does not tell Taylor what to do. It tells Taylor what kind of problem this actually is.

Taylor who was hired into it

Taylor accepts an operations role at a twelve-person technology company. The job posting described a structured environment—defined responsibilities, a clear reporting line, an established team. The interview involved the CEO, a department head, and two team members. The offer was formal, and the compensation was competitive.

The first week reveals a different picture. There is no onboarding documentation. The role Taylor was hired for turns out to overlap significantly with two other people's responsibilities, and the boundaries have never been formally established. The authority structure that appeared on the organizational chart is largely aspirational; most decisions route back to the CEO regardless of what the chart suggests. The processes referenced during the interview are either in early development or exist only as intentions.

Taylor's first interpretation: He is still finding his footing. New environment. Give it time. Work harder, fill the gaps, demonstrate value.

Three months in, Taylor has built several informal processes, absorbed significant operational risk, and taken on responsibilities that were never part of the original role description. The CEO is enthusiastic. There is still no evaluation framework, no defined authority structure, and no institutional mechanism for any of what Taylor has been carrying.

Taylor was not hired into a structured organization that needed improvement. Taylor was hired into The Nothing and began doing what capable people do when they land there, which is compensating for the structural conditions without naming them first.

The classification changes the response. Taylor is not failing to adapt to a Tier 2 environment. Taylor is operating in Tier 3, and the question is no longer how to navigate the structure but whether to build it and on what terms.

◆ ◆ ◆

What The Nothing Is Not

Before leaving this chapter, one clarification matters.

The Nothing is not a judgment. It is a structural classification. Describing Tier 3 as the absence of organizational structure is not the same as saying that people operating in Tier 3 are failing, or that entrepreneurship is a mistake, or that the veteran who was hired into The Nothing made a wrong decision.

Some of the most capable, disciplined, and ultimately successful people operate in Tier 3. What they share is not immunity from its conditions; it is awareness of them. They know what The Nothing does not provide. They build what it does not give them. They evaluate themselves against criteria they construct deliberately rather than waiting for criteria that will never arrive on their own.

The same is true for veterans hired into Tier 3. The ones who navigate it effectively are not the ones who work hardest or complain least. They are the ones who name where they are accurately and then decide, with clear eyes, whether to build the structural layer the organization is missing, negotiate for it explicitly, or move toward an environment that already has it.

The framework does not tell you to avoid Tier 3. It tells you to enter it—or recognize that you are already in it—with accurate information. That is what structural literacy makes possible. Not the avoidance of hard terrain. Accurate navigation of it.

What Comes Next

You now have the full picture.

You know what you came from—the most bounded system in modern society—and why its structural conditions shaped your expectations in ways you may never have had reason to name before.

You know what you walked into or what you may one day walk into. The three tiers. The structural containment spectrum. The four observable conditions that tell you what kind of system you are actually dealing with.

You know how systems are lived through situations and how to read a specific moment as structural data rather than a personal signal.

And you know The Nothing. What it is. What it is not. How you get there, by choice or by accident. What it does over time. How to recognize it.

What you do not yet have is the operational tool—the method for running that diagnosis systematically, in any environment, in real time.

That is what the next chapter delivers.

The pattern described in this chapter—early momentum, concentration fracture, effort escalation, identity erosion—reflects consistent accounts from veterans who entered Tier 3 by both paths. The absence of structural feedback is particularly well-documented as a source of post-separation disorientation for veterans accustomed to codified evaluation systems. Building evaluation criteria deliberately is the primary structural intervention available to veterans operating in Tier 3.

PART FIVE

The Diagnostic Method

CHAPTER 9

THE DIAGNOSTIC METHOD: HOW TO CLASSIFY ANY ENVIRONMENT

◆ ◆ ◆

Everything in this book has been building toward a single operational capability: the ability to walk into any environment and classify it accurately. This chapter delivers the tool—the seven-step Civilian Systems Diagnostic Method. It explains each step in full, identifies the four conditions you are always reading, and names the five most common misreadings that cause the method to produce inaccurate results.

◆ ◆ ◆

Key Terms

Civilian Systems Diagnostic Method: The operational component of the Applied Systems Transition Framework. A seven-step repeating loop for classifying any civilian environment by its structural conditions. Designed for use in real conditions, with incomplete information, under the time constraints of an actual transition.

Position markers: The specific observable indicators that reveal where an organization sits on the structural containment spectrum. Drawn from the four conditions: authority, roles, risk, and evaluation.

Structural misattribution (reverse): The error of attributing structural outcomes to individual causes when assessing an environment—the mirror image of attributing personal outcomes to structural causes.

Re-evaluation: Step 7 of the diagnostic loop. The recognition that structural conditions are dynamic and that an accurate classification requires periodic confirmation against new observations.

◆ ◆ ◆

Everything in this book has been building toward a single capability.

Not an understanding of military structure. You already had that. Not a general awareness that civilian organizations differ from the military. You felt that the moment you arrived. And not a vocabulary for describing what you were experiencing, though the framework gives you that too.

What this book has been building toward is the ability to walk into any environment—a job interview, a first week, an organization you are considering joining, one you have been inside for months—and classify it accurately. To read the structural signals that are present in every environment, interpret what they mean, and draw a conclusion that is grounded in evidence rather than assumption.

That capability is now within reach. This chapter makes it operational.

The Civilian Systems Diagnostic Method is a seven-step loop. It is not a checklist to complete once and file away. It is a repeating process, one that you run continuously as new information arrives and re-run whenever the environment changes or your initial classification stops explaining what you are observing.

It is designed to be used in real conditions, with incomplete information, under the time constraints of an actual transition. Not in a classroom. Not in hindsight. In the moment, with whatever you can observe from where you are standing.

◆ ◆ ◆

The Four Conditions You Are Always Reading

Before the steps, here's a reminder of what you are reading for. Every environment you enter contains four observable structural conditions.

- Where authority lives.
- How roles are defined.
- How risk is distributed.
- How outcomes are evaluated.

Those four conditions are the structural signal underneath every situation you encounter. The diagnostic method gives you a disciplined way to surface them rather than letting the situation's surface content obscure them.

◆ ◆ ◆

The Seven-Step Diagnostic Loop

Step 1 — Identify the environment

Before you can read a system, you need to define what system you are reading. This sounds obvious. But it is frequently skipped, and skipping it produces misclassification before the diagnostic has begun.

Identifying the environment means naming what you are actually assessing. Not the industry. Not the job title. The specific organizational unit you are operating inside or evaluating. A federal agency and a federal contractor are not the same environment, even if they occupy the same building. A growing startup and an established mid-sized firm are not the same environment, even if they operate in the same sector.

Be specific. Name the organization. Name the unit or team within it, if that is the level you are assessing. The more precisely you define the environment, the more accurately the rest of the diagnostic will run.

Step 2 — Observe situations

You do not observe systems directly. You observe situations, and situations are where structural signals appear.

At this step, you are collecting raw data. What has happened? What was said? What was the outcome? Who was involved? What did the process look like? You are not yet interpreting. You are not drawing conclusions yet. You are accumulating observations.

The situations most likely to produce useful structural signals were covered in chapter 5: the interview process, the first ninety days, decisions that do or do not get made, and feedback that does or does not arrive. But structural signals appear in every interaction. A meeting. An email. A conversation about a project. A request for resources. How the organization responds to a problem. How it responds to a success.

Collect as many observations as the environment and timeline allow. A single situation is rarely enough for an accurate classification. A pattern across multiple situations is.

Step 3 — Identify signals

Not every observation contains a structural signal. Some outcomes are personal. Some are coincidental. Some are produced by individual behavior rather than structural conditions.

At this step, you are sorting your observations. Which ones point toward something structural, something that would likely produce the same outcome regardless of who was at the center of it? Which ones are more plausibly explained by individual behavior, specific circumstances, or factors that are not structural in nature?

The signal identification step is where structural misattribution is most likely to occur in reverse. Where veterans, trained to take personal accountability, attribute structural outcomes to individual causes. The discipline here is to hold the observation open long enough to ask, "Would this situation have produced the same outcome for a different person in the same position?" If the answer is probably yes, you are looking at a structural signal.

Step 4 — Interpret position markers

Position markers are the specific observable indicators that tell you where an organization sits on the structural containment spectrum. They are the evidence you use to make a classification.

Authority markers: Can you trace who owns a decision? Is that traceable through formal documentation or only through informal knowledge held by people who have been there long enough to learn it? When a decision needs to be made, does it get made, or does it circulate?

Role markers: Did the role exist before you arrived—documented, defined, with established expectations? Or did it emerge through the work, shaped by the person doing it and the organization's evolving needs? Are the boundaries of your role clear, or do they depend on negotiation and context?

Risk markers: When something goes wrong, where does the exposure land? Does the organization have mechanisms—processes, oversight, corrective action—that absorb a share of it? Or does it land directly on the individual with nothing underneath?

Evaluation markers: Were the criteria for good performance established before the work began? Are they documented and applied consistently? Or are they retrospective, defined by outcomes after the fact, interpreted through relationships, and rarely tied to standards that were stated in advance?

Read the markers that your observations have surfaced. Not every marker will be visible in every situation. Use what you have.

Step 5 — Classify structural conditions

This is the classification step. Based on the position markers you have interpreted, where does this environment sit on the structural containment spectrum?

Tier 1 — Bounded: Authority is explicit and traceable. Roles are predefined and documented. Evaluation criteria exist in advance. The institution absorbs significant risk on behalf of the people operating inside it.

Tier 2 — Unbounded: Structure exists but is incomplete, inconsistently applied, or unevenly distributed. Authority operates partly through formal channels and partly through informal ones. Roles are defined but shift. Evaluation happens, but criteria are not always established in advance. Risk is partially absorbed and partially carried by individuals.

Tier 3 — The Nothing: No stable authority. No predefined roles. No evaluation framework that exists in advance. No institutional risk absorption. The complete absence of organizational structure, whether the organization is one you built or one you were hired into.

Most real organizations sit between the markers. Classify to the tier that best describes the dominant structural conditions and note where the organization is closer to the boundary than the center.

Step 6 — Identify implications

A classification without implications is an academic exercise. This step converts the classification into actionable intelligence.

What does this tier tell you about how to operate effectively in this environment? A Tier 1 classification tells you that authority is traceable. Use the formal chain and document your interactions with it. A Tier 2 classification tells you that authority operates informally as often as formally. Identify where the real decision-making lives before you need a decision. A Tier 3 classification tells you that the structural conditions you need do not exist yet. Decide which ones you will build, which ones you will negotiate for, and which ones you will absorb personally.

What does this tier tell you about risk? In Tier 1, the institution absorbs a significant share. You can operate with the confidence that not every error becomes a personal catastrophe. In Tier 2, risk is unevenly distributed. Identify where institutional absorption ends and personal exposure begins before you take on significant responsibility. In Tier 3, all risk is personal. Price it into every decision before you make it.

What does this tier tell you about evaluation? In Tier 1, evaluation criteria likely exist in advance. Find them and perform against them explicitly. In Tier 2, criteria may be informal or retrospective. Establish your own in advance and make them visible to the people who will evaluate you. In Tier 3, no criteria exist until you build them. Build them deliberately and communicate them to anyone whose assessment of your work matters.

The implications step is where the classification becomes useful in practice. Do not skip it.

Step 7 — Re-evaluate

The classification you make today is accurate for today. Organizations change. Tier positions shift. A startup that builds governance architecture moves from Tier 3 toward Tier 2. A large organization that loses key structure through rapid growth or leadership turnover can slide from Tier 1 toward Tier 2. A Tier 2 organization in a period of stability can tighten toward Tier 1 in specific functions.

Re-evaluation is not a sign that the initial classification was wrong. It is a recognition that structural conditions are dynamic and that an accurate classification requires periodic confirmation against new observations.

Re-evaluate when something changes significantly in the organization's leadership, funding, or size. When your observations stop matching your classification. When a situation produces an outcome that your current classification cannot explain. When you are making a crucial decision that depends on the classification being accurate.

The loop does not close. It continues.

◆ ◆ ◆

Common Misreadings

The diagnostic method is a tool, and like any tool, it can be applied incorrectly. These are the misreadings that appear most often.

Classifying by industry instead of structure

The most common misreading is using industry as a proxy for tier. Federal agencies are assumed to be Tier 1. Startups are assumed to be Tier 3. Large corporations are assumed to be Tier 1 or upper Tier 2.

None of those assumptions are reliable.

Federal or state agencies that have been defunded, reorganized, or left without stable leadership may have the legal architecture of Tier 1 and the functional reality of Tier 2. The position classifications exist on paper. The performance standards are documented somewhere. But if the authority chain is unclear, resources are inconsistent, roles have been collapsed or left vacant, and evaluation cycles are not functioning as designed, the structural experience of working there is Tier 2 regardless of the agency's federal status. The structure exists in regulation. It may not exist in practice.

A well-capitalized startup with formal governance, documented processes, and institutional investors may function as upper Tier 2 despite its age. A federal contractor operating under minimal oversight in a loosely governed program may function as Tier 2 despite its federal affiliation.

Industry is a starting hypothesis, not a classification. Classify based on observed structural conditions, not assumed ones.

Classifying too early

A single observation is rarely sufficient for an accurate classification. Veterans accustomed to rapid assessment under pressure sometimes classify after the first interaction—the interview, the first week—and then filter all subsequent observations through that initial classification rather than updating it.

Early classification is a hypothesis. Hold it loosely. Continue observing. Update when the evidence warrants it.

Confusing management quality with structural tier

A well-managed Tier 2 organization can feel like Tier 1 because the leadership is skilled at compensating for structural gaps. A poorly managed Tier 1 organization can feel like Tier 2 because the leadership is failing to use the structural resources available to it.

The classification is about structural conditions, not management quality. Ask what the structure provides, not how well the current leadership is performing within it.

Treating the classification as permanent

Organizations move. A classification that was accurate at hire may not be accurate eighteen months later. Veterans who classified their environment accurately on entry and then stopped re-evaluating sometimes find themselves operating on outdated structural assumptions, navigating an organization that has moved significantly from where it was when they arrived.

Build re-evaluation into your practice. The classification is a current reading, not a permanent label.

Using the classification as a reason not to act

The diagnostic method identifies structural conditions. It does not excuse inaction inside them. A Tier 2 classification explains why authority is inconsistent. It does not mean you stop working to find where authority actually lives. A Tier 3 classification explains why evaluation criteria are absent. It does not mean you stop performing or stop building the criteria you need.

The classification is a starting point for a more accurate response. It is not a verdict.

◆ ◆ ◆

What Comes Next

The method is now in your hands. The next chapter puts it to work. Taylor runs the full seven-step diagnostic across three real environments simultaneously, arriving at three different classifications, each one producing a separate set of implications and a diverse set of decisions. Then the diagnostic reference card gives you the method in condensed, field-usable form.

The seven-step diagnostic loop draws on established principles from organizational analysis and systems classification research. The four structural conditions—authority, roles, risk, and evaluation—reflect dimensions documented across organizational behavior literature as the primary determinants of institutional structure. The application to veteran transition is original to this framework.

CHAPTER 10

THE DIAGNOSTIC IN ACTION: THREE ENVIRONMENTS, ONE METHOD

◆ ◆ ◆

The diagnostic method is not a framework to study. It is a tool to use. This chapter shows Taylor running the full seven-step loop across three environments simultaneously—a federal agency, a mid-sized nonprofit, and an early-stage technology company—arriving at three different classifications, each producing a distinct set of implications. The chapter closes with the one-page diagnostic reference card.

◆ ◆ ◆

Taylor Runs the Full Diagnostic

Taylor is a logistics and operations specialist. The branch does not matter. The years of service do not matter. What matters is that Taylor applies the same method to all three environments and arrives at three different classifications.

Environment one: the federal agency

Step 1 — Identify the environment

A regional office of a large federal agency, approximately two hundred staff, operating under established federal employment law and Office of Personnel Management guidelines.

Step 2 — Observe situations

The interview process involved a structured panel with pre-submitted questions. A formal offer was issued through an HR system. Onboarding documentation was sent before the start date. During the interview, the hiring manager referenced specific performance standards by name.

Step 3 — Identify signals

The pre-submitted questions signal predefined evaluation criteria. The formal HR process signals institutional structure. The referenced performance standards signal that evaluation criteria exist in advance. These are structural signals, not individual ones.

Step 4 — Interpret position markers

Authority appears traceable through formal documentation. The role existed before Taylor applied. It was posted with a GS classification and documented responsibilities. Risk appears institutionally absorbed. The organization has established processes for performance management and corrective action. Evaluation criteria were named before the work began.

Step 5 — Classify

Tier 1 — Bounded. The structural signals are consistent and point clearly toward the high-containment end of the spectrum.

Step 6 — Identify implications

The authority chain is usable. Document interactions with it and use formal channels for decisions that require institutional backing. Evaluation criteria exist in advance. Find them, understand them, and perform against them explicitly. The gap between military Tier 1 and civilian Tier 1 still exists. The pace, the mission, and the culture will differ, but the structural signals are the most familiar Taylor will find in a civilian environment.

Step 7 — Re-evaluate

Confirm the classification after ninety days of direct observation. Federal agencies can have significant structural variation across offices and programs. The regional office may have more or less structural consistency than the parent agency.

Environment two: the mid-sized nonprofit

Step 1 — Identify the environment

A regional nonprofit with approximately forty staff, operating in workforce development, funded primarily through government grants and foundation support.

Step 2 — Observe situations

The interview was conversational rather than structured. The job description was detailed, but the hiring manager indicated the role would evolve. Onboarding was described as informal. When Taylor asked about performance review cycles, the response was positive but vague: "We do check-ins. We're pretty flexible about how that works."

Step 3 — Identify signals

The conversational interview signals that evaluation criteria may not have been predefined. The evolving role description signals that role boundaries are not fixed. The vague response to the performance review question signals that the evaluation framework may be informal or inconsistently applied. These are structural signals.

Step 4 — Interpret position markers

Authority is not yet visible. The hiring manager's reference to "checking in with the team" suggests informal consensus may operate alongside formal authority. The role is defined but described as evolving, which signals Tier 2 role flexibility. The grant-funded model suggests that financial risk is partially externalized, but that program continuity depends on funding renewal, a structural risk condition that sits partly with the institution and partly with individuals.

Step 5 — Classify

Tier 2 — Unbounded. Structure exists, but is incomplete and inconsistently applied. The signals are consistent with a mid-sized organization operating under resource and flexibility constraints that make full structural containment difficult to maintain.

Step 6 — Identify implications

Locate where authority actually lives before needing a decision. The formal title may not reflect the real decision-making structure. Establish personal evaluation criteria in advance and make them visible to the director. Understand the grant cycle and what program continuity depends on. That is where institutional risk absorption ends and personal exposure begins. Tier 2 is navigable, but it requires more active structural awareness than Tier 1.

Step 7 — Re-evaluate

The classification should be confirmed after sixty days of direct observation. Nonprofits can vary significantly in structural consistency depending on leadership tenure, board engagement, and funding stability. A new executive director or a significant grant loss can shift a Tier 2 nonprofit toward Tier 3 quickly.

Environment three: the early-stage technology company

Step 1 — Identify the environment

A technology startup, eighteen months old, eight full-time staff, founder-led, pre-revenue with active investor funding.

Step 2 — Observe situations

The interview was a series of informal conversations with the founder and two team members. No formal job description was provided. The role was described verbally as "operations and whatever else we need." Onboarding was described as "You'll figure it out pretty quickly; we're a small team." When Taylor asked about performance review processes, the founder laughed and said they had not built that yet.

Step 3 — Identify signals

The absence of a formal job description signals no predefined role. The "whatever else we need" framing signals that role boundaries will be determined by organizational need rather than established in advance. The explicit statement that performance review processes have not been built signals no evaluation framework. The founder's laugh signals that this absence is accepted as a feature of the environment, not recognized as a gap. These are structural signals, and they are pointing in a consistent direction.

Step 4 — Interpret position markers

Authority lives with the founder, entirely and informally. No role exists before Taylor arrives. No evaluation framework exists. All risk is personal. The company has investor funding but no institutional mechanisms to absorb operational or performance risk on behalf of employees. The structural conditions of Tier 3 are present across all four markers.

Step 5 — Classify

Tier 3 — The Nothing. The signals are unambiguous. This is not a weak Tier 2. It is the absence of organizational structure.

Step 6 — Identify implications

Every structural condition this environment needs will require construction. If Taylor accepts this role, the work includes both doing the job and building the framework the job needs to function in simultaneously, without institutional support underneath. The risk exposure is total and personal. Before accepting, Taylor needs to answer three questions: What structural conditions am I willing to build? What am I willing to carry personally? And is the upside of this environment sufficient to justify the structural exposure it requires?

Step 7 — Re-evaluate

Early-stage organizations move quickly. A Tier 3 classification today can shift toward Tier 2 within six to twelve months if the organization builds governance architecture deliberately. Re-evaluate at ninety days and at every significant organizational change—new funding, new hires at the leadership level, formalization of any structural process.

Three environments. One method. Three different classifications. Each one producing a separate set of implications, a different navigation approach, and a separate set of questions Taylor needs to answer before deciding.

◆ ◆ ◆

What to Do with a Classification — and What Not to Do

A classification is the beginning of a response, not the end of one.

What to do: Use the classification to calibrate your expectations before they form against the wrong baseline. Use it to identify which structural conditions you can rely on and which ones you will need to build or compensate for yourself. Use it to locate where authority actually lives, how risk is actually distributed, and how evaluation actually works before you need that information in a high-stakes moment.

Use it to make better decisions. Not just employment decisions, but decisions inside the environment you are already in. A Tier 2 classification changes how you navigate authority. A Tier 3 classification changes what you build. A Tier 1 classification tells you which structural resources are available to you and how to use them.

What not to do: Do not use the classification as a reason to disengage. A Tier 2 classification is not a verdict that the organization is broken. A Tier 3 classification is not a reason to leave immediately. The classification tells you what kind of terrain you are in. What you do with that terrain is a separate decision.

Do not use the classification to justify assumptions about people. Structural conditions produce outcomes, but the people operating inside those conditions are not the conditions themselves. A manager in a Tier 2 organization who fails to deliver consistent feedback is operating inside a structural feedback environment that does not require it of them. That is information about the structure. It is not a character assessment.

And do not treat the classification as final. The loop continues. New information updates the classification. The re-evaluation step is not optional.

CIVILIAN SYSTEMS DIAGNOSTIC CARD

Applied Systems Transition Framework · Dr. Paul Encinias, EdD

THE FOUR CONDITIONS

Authority: Where does it live? Can you trace it? Does formal match actual?

Roles: Did the role exist before you arrived? Are boundaries defined or emergent?

Risk: Where does exposure land when something goes wrong? Institution or individual?

Evaluation: Were criteria defined before the work began? Are they applied consistently?

THE SEVEN STEPS

1. Identify the environment — name the specific organizational unit
2. Observe situations — collect raw data from interactions and outcomes
3. Identify signals — sort structural from personal or coincidental
4. Interpret position markers — read authority, roles, risk, evaluation
5. Classify structural conditions — Tier 1, Tier 2, or Tier 3
6. Identify implications — what does the classification tell you?
7. Re-evaluate — update when the environment changes

THE THREE TIERS

Tier 1 — Bounded: Explicit authority. Predefined roles. Advance criteria. Institutional risk absorption.

Tier 2 — Unbounded: Partial, inconsistent structure. Authority partly informal. Risk shared.

Tier 3 — The Nothing: No stable authority. No defined roles. No evaluation framework. No institutional risk absorption.

THE KEY QUESTION

Is this about me—or about the system I am in?

© 2026 Paul Encinias. All rights reserved. From the *Civilian Orientation Manual*, Volume I. Unauthorized reproduction prohibited.

Cut along lines · Fold in half · Carry with you

◆ ◆ ◆

Mission Ready

You now have the tool. Not a framework to study in the abstract. Not a set of concepts to carry around without application. A method—a repeating, evidence-based, field-usable diagnostic process that you can run on any environment you encounter, starting today.

The question this book set out to answer was not whether you were capable. You were capable before you opened the first page. The question was what kind of system you were actually in and whether you had the structural literacy to read it accurately before making decisions inside it.

Job well done.

◆ ◆ ◆

What Comes Next

Volume I gave you one thing: the ability to look at any civilian environment and name what kind of system you are dealing with.

That ability changes everything that follows. Not because it solves the practical problems of transition—the resume, the interview, the income gap, the authority placement—but because it gives you an accurate foundation to work from before those problems are engaged.

Volume II is where the diagnostic becomes operational. If this volume taught you to read the environment, Volume II teaches you to move through it, giving you the tools to act with the same confidence you brought to military systems. The next volume is for operators.

The diagnostic method you now have is the prerequisite for all of it.

CLOSING

What This Gives You and What Comes Next

What You Can Do Now That You Could Not Do Before

Before this book, the friction of transition had explanations, but most of them were personal ones. You needed to adapt. You needed to learn civilian culture. You needed to translate your experience more effectively. You needed to be more patient, more flexible, more willing to start over. Some of that was true. None of it was the whole story.

The whole story is structural. The friction you felt—or the friction you are preparing to feel—can largely be attributed to the gap between the system you came from and the systems you are entering. That gap is real. It is observable. It follows patterns that repeat across every sector, every size, and every type of civilian organization. And it is readable once you have the framework to read it.

You now have that framework.

You can look at any civilian environment and identify the four observable structural conditions that tell you what kind of system you are actually dealing with. You can classify that environment as Tier 1, Tier 2, or Tier 3: not based on assumption or industry but based on evidence. You can read specific situations for the structural signals they contain rather than defaulting to a personal explanation before the structural one has been considered. You can run the seven-step diagnostic in real time, with incomplete information, under the conditions of an actual transition.

And you can ask the question that changes everything before you draw a conclusion:

Is this about me—or about the system I am in?

That question and the structural literacy behind it are what this book delivers. It is not a small thing.

◆ ◆ ◆

What This Book Does Not Give You — and Why That Is Intentional

This book does not tell you where to work. It does not recommend specific employers, career paths, industries, or timelines. It does not promise that structural literacy will eliminate transition friction. It will not. It does not guarantee outcomes.

What it gives you is a more accurate foundation for every decision that follows. What you build on that foundation is yours to determine.

This book also does not give you the applied tools. It does not show you how to read a job posting for structural signals, how to use an interview to gather diagnostic data while also performing in it, how to negotiate compensation with an accurate understanding of how risk and value are distributed in the environment you are entering, or how to position yourself for authority in an organization once you understand where authority actually lives.

Those tools exist. They are the subject of Volume II. This book is the prerequisite for them because, without accurate structural classification, the applied tools operate on a faulty foundation. You cannot effectively negotiate your position in a system you have not correctly identified.

Volume I gives you the diagnostic. Volume II gives you the instruments. Volume III gives you the complete reference system—institutional-grade, cross-referenced, designed for repeated use across the full arc of a civilian career.

You are at the beginning of that arc, not the end of it.

One More Variable You Need to Read

There is a variable reshaping civilian environments faster than any other right now, and it belongs in this framework before you close this book.

Artificial intelligence is not a technology story. It is a structural one. When an organization adopts AI tools aggressively—automating defined roles, shifting decision authority to systems, changing how performance is measured and by whom—it is moving the four observable conditions. Authority relocates. Roles dissolve or consolidate. Risk redistributes. Evaluation criteria change, sometimes overnight. An organization you classified as Tier 1 six months ago may be operating as Tier 2 today. A Tier 2 environment absorbing AI-driven restructuring can slide toward The Nothing faster than any other force currently in the civilian landscape.

This does not require a new framework. It requires the one you already have, applied more frequently. When you are evaluating a new environment—or re-evaluating one you are already in—look for AI adoption as a structural signal, not a technical detail. Ask where authority is moving. Ask whether roles are still defined the way they were when you arrived. Ask how outcomes are now being evaluated and based on what. The diagnostic method was built for changing conditions. AI is a change in conditions. Run the loop. Volume II addresses this directly, including how to read AIrestructured environments when you are inside them and how to make applied decisions.

◆ ◆ ◆

This Does Not Just Affect You

There is something this book has not yet said directly. It needs to be said before you close it.

You are not the only one living this transition.

Your spouse or partner has been living it too. They watched you leave a system that defined nearly every parameter of your shared life—where you lived, how you planned, what stability looked like, what the future was allowed to look like. They watched you enter civilian environments that did not behave the way either of you expected. They absorbed the financial pressure when the income gap was real. They absorbed the relational pressure when the structural disorientation came home with you at the end of the day. They tried to help without a framework for what was actually happening.

Your children lived it too. In the moves, in the school changes, in the periods of instability that no one in the family had a vocabulary for. Children do not understand structural containment. But they feel its absence. They feel the difference between a household anchored by institutional certainty and one navigating a system that keeps shifting underneath it.

The structural misattribution that this book addresses does not stay at the office. It comes home. When a veteran interprets a system-produced outcome as personal failure, that interpretation does not disappear at the end of the workday. It shapes how they talk about their work, how they assess their own value, how much of their energy is consumed by a problem that was never personal to begin with. The family absorbs all of that without ever having been briefed on the structural conditions producing it.

That is not a small thing. For many veteran families, the transition period is the hardest sustained period of their shared life. Not because the veteran failed. Not because the family failed. Because everyone was navigating a structural problem without a structural framework, and the gap between what was expected and what was found had no name.

This framework gives it a name.

If you have a partner, consider sharing what this book gave you. Not the vocabulary, the understanding. The core idea that the friction was structural, not personal. That you were not failing to adapt. That the system was built differently, for different purposes, under different constraints. And that the disorientation both of you felt was a reasonable response to a real structural gap, not evidence of inadequacy on anyone's part.

That conversation—the one where the transition stops being a personal story and becomes a structural one—changes things. It changes how the family understands what happened. It changes how they support what comes next. And it changes what the veteran is carrying alone that does not need to be carried alone.

Structural literacy is not just a professional tool. For veteran families, it is a shared language for one of the hardest chapters of a shared life.

◆ ◆ ◆

The Next Set of Problems

Volume I addressed one problem: the absence of structural literacy at the point of transition. That problem is now addressed.

The next set of problems is applied. Resumes that fail not because the experience is weak but because the translation is structurally misaligned.

Interviews that underperform, not because the candidate is unprepared, but because the structural signals in the room are being misread. Income gaps that persist not because the value is not there but because the negotiation is happening without an accurate understanding of how risk and value are distributed in the target environment. Authority placement failures that repeat across organizations, not because the veteran lacks leadership capacity, but because the authority structure of each new environment is being navigated on assumption rather than diagnosis.

Those are solvable problems. They are the subject of Volume II.

The diagnostic method you now have is the prerequisite for solving them. Use it. Run it on every environment you encounter. Update it as new information arrives. Share it with the people navigating this transition alongside you.

The question was never whether you were capable.

The question was what kind of system you were actually in.

Now you can answer it.

ABOUT THE AUTHOR

◆ ◆ ◆

Dr. Paul Encinias is a systems researcher with more than ten years of research experience and fifteen years of applied experience studying how people navigate complex systems.

He earned a Doctor of Education in Organizational Leadership from the University of Massachusetts Global and an MBA with a concentration in international business. He also completed advanced graduate studies in executive and nonprofit leadership. He is currently attending Law, pursuing a Master of Legal Studies in Litigation.

His work examines the gap between military and civilian institutional systems and the ways that misunderstanding that gap shapes individual decisions, stability, and long-term outcomes. The *Civilian Orientation Manual* grows directly from that research, bringing together organizational leadership, quality management, and systems analysis. His doctoral research is among the first formal works to document the structural differences between military and civilian organizational environments.

A central purpose of his work is to use his education and experience to develop programs that support veterans during transition and help reduce the conditions that can lead to crisis and, in the worst cases, to suicide. He has seen where the gap leads when it goes unaddressed. That is why this manual exists.

Dr. Encinias also works as a quality management systems architect, designing structured systems that connect organizational processes, decision-making, and performance outcomes. He has extensive experience in government procurement.

His work has been recognized by the Department of the Navy, the United States Senate, the California State Legislature, the University of California Merced, the SBDC Regional Network, flag admirals, commanding officers, and other institutional leaders. He holds a certificate of special congressional recognition.

Dr. Encinias is a US Navy veteran who deployed in support of Operation Enduring Freedom in 2011.

ACKNOWLEDGMENTS

This book exists because of people, not just research. Over more than a decade of work, through the hard years and the good ones, a handful of people never wavered. This page is for them.

To my wife, Courtney. You have been beside me through every stage of this work, through the years when the direction was unclear and the years when the path finally became visible. You have seen the best of this process and the hardest parts of it, and you stayed. Everything in this book that required patience, belief, and endurance was made possible because of you. Thank you does not cover it, but it is where I start.

To my children, Greyson, Marcus, and Amelia. You are the reason the work matters. Watching you grow up gave the research its purpose. I hope one day you read this and understand what we were building and why.

To my mother, Josie. You believed in me before I had given you much evidence to work with, and you never stopped. That kind of belief is not a small thing. It carried more weight than you know, in more moments than I can count. Thank you.

To my father, Pete. You taught me to keep trying and to take calculated risks. That lesson is in this book in many ways. Thank you for modeling what it looks like to stay in the fight.

To my brother Pete and his wife Lara, and to Cruz, Aria, and Dazy. Thank you for the support and for being the kind of family that shows up. It matters more than it might seem from the outside.

To my sister, Genevieve. You have always helped when asked, without hesitation. That consistency is a form of love. Thank you.

To the professors, doctors, and universities who spent countless hours helping refine this research and providing guidance throughout the years, thank you. You saw the potential in this work before it was finished, and your investment in it made the difference between an innovative idea and a completed framework.

And to the veterans this book was written for—the ones navigating a transition that no one fully prepared them for—and the families living it alongside them. This is for you.

To the counselors, case workers, transition officers, peer support specialists, and nonprofit staff who show up every day for veterans and their families, often without enough resources, often without enough recognition. The gap this book describes is real, and you are standing in it, trying to help people across. That work matters.

Above all, to God, for the clarity to see the purpose in the hard years and the strength to see this through.

GLOSSARY

◆ ◆ ◆

Key terms used throughout this volume, drawn from chapters 3–9. Terms appear in the order they are introduced.

Chapter 3 — The Big Picture

Structural containment. The degree to which an organization provides predefined roles, codified authority, consistent evaluation criteria, and institutional risk absorption. The primary variable that distinguishes the three tiers from one another.

Tier 1 — Bounded. A civilian environment with explicit authority, predefined roles, advanced evaluation criteria, and significant institutional risk absorption. The most structurally coherent civilian tier.

Tier 2 — Unbounded. A civilian environment with a partial or unevenly applied structure. Authority, roles, and evaluation exist but operate inconsistently.

Tier 3 — The Nothing. The complete absence of organizational structure. No stable authority, predefined roles, advanced evaluation criteria, or institutional risk absorption.

Chapter 4 — The Three Tiers in Practice

Tier position. Where an organization sits on the structural containment spectrum at a given point in time. Tier position is dynamic and can shift as organizations grow, lose governance, or change operating conditions.

The spectrum. The full range of structural containment from fully bounded (Tier 1) to completely unstructured (Tier 3). Most organizations sit between the markers rather than at the extremes.

Chapter 5 — The Small Picture

Structural misattribution. The act of interpreting a system-produced outcome as a personal one. The most common and most costly error veterans make when reading civilian environments.

Structural literacy. The ability to pause in a specific situation and ask whether an outcome was produced by personal performance or by the structural conditions of the environment.

Surface content. The first layer of any situation: what was said, what happened, what the outcome was.

Structural signal. The second layer of any situation: what the outcome reveals about how authority, roles, risk, and evaluation actually operate in that environment.

Chapter 6 — Reading the Signal

The diagnostic question. "Is this about me—or about the system I am in?" The habit that converts structural literacy from a concept into a practice.

Compliance process. A hiring or evaluation process conducted to satisfy procedural requirements rather than to produce a genuine selection.

Chapter 7 — The Nothing

The chosen path. Entry into Tier 3 through deliberate choice: entrepreneurship, consulting, or self-employment.

The accidental path. Entry into Tier 3 through a hiring process that presented the organization as more structured than it actually was.

Institutional floor. The baseline of structural support that military service always provided—risk absorption, evaluation framework, authority continuity—even in austere operating environments.

Chapter 8 — What The Nothing Does

Concentration risk. The condition in which revenue, relationships, or institutional knowledge is held in a single source.

Structural feedback. The institutional signals that tell an operator whether effort is building toward something durable.

Role-person fusion. The condition in which no boundary exists between the work and the individual doing it.

Chapter 9 — The Diagnostic Method

Civilian Systems Diagnostic Method. A seven-step repeating loop for classifying any civilian environment by its structural conditions.

Position markers. The specific observable indicators that reveal where an organization sits on the structural containment spectrum.

Re-evaluation. Step 7 of the diagnostic loop. The recognition that structural conditions are dynamic and that an accurate classification requires periodic confirmation against new observations.

RESOURCES

The following organizations and programs provide direct support to veterans, service members, and their families. Information is current at the time of publication and subject to change.

Crisis Support

Veterans Crisis Line. Dial 988, then press 1. Chat at VeteransCrisisLine.net/Chat. Text 838255. Available 24 hours a day, 7 days a week. Confidential support for veterans, service members, and their families in crisis. (988 also serves all individuals in crisis; press 1 for dedicated veteran support).

Transition and Employment

American Job Centers. Employment assistance, job search resources, and transition support for veterans. Locations nationwide at careeronestop.org.

Transition Assistance Program (TAP). Department of Defense preseparation program providing employment assistance, benefits information, and transition planning. Available through the installation of Family Support Centers.

USAJOBS. Official federal government employment site. Veterans' preference and veteran-specific hiring authorities apply (usajobs.gov).

Regular Military Compensation (RMC) Calculator. Department of Defense tool for calculating total military compensation, including basic pay, housing allowance, subsistence allowance, and federal tax advantage. Use during transition to establish an accurate civilian salary equivalent before negotiating offers (militarypay.defense.gov/Calculators.aspx)

Benefits and Services

US Department of Veterans Affairs (VA). Full range of benefits including healthcare, disability compensation, education, and home loans. Visit va.gov or call 1-800-698-2411.

Veterans Service Organizations (VSOs). VA-recognized organizations that provide free claims assistance and advocacy. The VA works closely with the American Legion, VFW, DAV, and AMVETS. Find accredited VSOs at va.gov/ogc/apps/accreditation.

eBenefits. Online portal for managing VA benefits and military records (ebenefits.va.gov).

Entrepreneurship

Small Business Administration: Boots to Business. Entrepreneurship education program for transitioning service members and veterans (sba.gov/offices/headquarters/ovbd).

Mental Health and Family Support

Military OneSource. Free counseling, financial consultation, and support services for service members and families. Visit militaryonesource.mil or call 1-800-342-9647.

NOTES

Use these pages to record diagnostic observations, tier classifications, and structural signals as you encounter them.

NOTES

Use these pages to record diagnostic observations, tier classifications, and structural signals as you encounter them.

NOTES

Use these pages to record diagnostic observations, tier classifications, and structural signals as you encounter them.

Notes

Use these pages to record diagnostic observations, tier classifications, and structural signals as you encounter them.

Notes

Use these pages to record diagnostic observations, tier classifications, and structural signals as you encounter them.

Made in the USA
Coppell, TX
23 July 2026

84861262R00079